Nashville Travel Guide

BnW Travel Series

Ashok Kumawat

© 2023 Ashok Kumawat. All rights reserved.

Disclaimer: The information provided in this Nashville travel guide is intended for general reference purposes only. While every effort has been made to ensure the accuracy and reliability of the information, the dynamic nature of travel destinations means that some details may change over time. The author and publisher of this guide cannot be held responsible for any errors, omissions, or outdated information. It is recommended that readers verify important details such as opening hours, prices, and availability of attractions, accommodations, and services before making any travel arrangements. Readers are also advised to exercise caution and follow local laws, regulations, and safety guidelines during their visit. Travelers are encouraged to consult official websites, local tourism authorities, and other reliable sources for the most up-to-date and accurate information.

Table of contents:
- Introduction to Nashville: Music City USA
- Planning Your Nashville Adventure
- Getting Around: Transportation in Nashville
- Where to Stay: Accommodation Options
- Best Time to Visit Nashville
- Exploring Downtown Nashville
- The Music Scene: Honky Tonks and Live Music Venues
- Nashville's Historic Landmarks and Museums
- Discovering Nashville's Neighborhoods
- Family-Friendly Activities in Nashville
- Outdoor Adventures in and around the City
- Shopping in Music City: Unique Boutiques and Malls
- Dining Experiences: Southern Cuisine and Beyond
- Nashville's Craft Beer and Distillery Scene
- Exploring Nashville's Parks and Green Spaces
- Day Trips from Nashville: Nearby Attractions
- Sports and Entertainment in Nashville
- Art and Culture: Galleries and Artistic Spaces
- Music History and Heritage in Nashville
- LGBTQ+ Nashville: A Vibrant Community
- Honoring Civil Rights: Nashville's Significance
- Nashville's Architectural Gems
- Events and Festivals: Celebrating Music and Culture
- Discovering Nashville's Coffee Culture
- Wellness and Relaxation: Spas and Retreats
- Uncovering Nashville's Haunted Places
- Volunteer Opportunities in Nashville
- Shopping for Souvenirs: Unique Nashville Gifts
- Hidden Gems and Off-the-Beaten-Path Destinations
- Tips for Traveling with Pets in Nashville
- Music Recording Studios and Music Industry Insights
- Exploring Nashville's Riverfront and Waterways
- Honoring Legendary Artists: Museums and Memorials
- Discovering Nashville's Literary Heritage
- Saying Goodbye to Nashville: Reflections and Memories

Introduction to Nashville: Music City USA

Nashville, also known as "Music City USA," is a vibrant and culturally rich destination that has captivated the hearts of visitors from around the world. Located in the state of Tennessee, Nashville is famous for its thriving music scene, southern hospitality, and historic landmarks. Whether you're a music enthusiast, a food lover, an outdoor adventurer, or a history buff, Nashville offers a wide array of experiences to suit every taste and interest.

One of the main reasons why Nashville earned its nickname is its deep-rooted connection to music. Renowned as the birthplace of country music, the city boasts a rich musical heritage that stretches back decades. From iconic venues like the Grand Ole Opry, Ryman Auditorium, and Bluebird Cafe to the bustling honky-tonks on Lower Broadway, live music is an integral part of Nashville's DNA. Visitors can immerse themselves in the sounds of country, bluegrass, rock, and various other genres as they explore the city's vibrant music scene.

Beyond its musical offerings, Nashville is a city steeped in history and culture. The city's historic landmarks, such as The Hermitage (home of President Andrew Jackson), Belle Meade Plantation, and the Parthenon in Centennial Park, provide glimpses into Nashville's past. These sites offer fascinating insights into the city's architectural beauty, rich heritage, and influential figures who shaped its development.

Nashville's neighborhoods each have their own distinct personality and charm, contributing to the city's diverse cultural fabric. Downtown Nashville is a bustling hub of activity, offering a mix of trendy bars, restaurants, and shops, as well as iconic attractions like the Country Music Hall of Fame and Museum. Midtown and the Gulch neighborhoods are known for their vibrant nightlife, while East Nashville has a bohemian vibe with its indie music venues, art galleries, and local eateries. Exploring these neighborhoods allows visitors to uncover the different facets of Nashville's character and experience its unique atmosphere.

Food enthusiasts will find Nashville to be a culinary paradise. The city is renowned for its delectable Southern cuisine, with iconic dishes like hot chicken and biscuits stealing the spotlight. From renowned barbecue joints to fine dining establishments and food trucks, Nashville offers a diverse range of culinary experiences to satisfy every palate. Visitors can indulge in soulful comfort food, sample locally brewed beers, or savor inventive creations from award-winning chefs.

For those seeking outdoor adventures, Nashville has plenty to offer. The city is surrounded by stunning natural beauty, including nearby parks, lakes, and hiking trails. Radnor Lake

State Park provides a serene retreat for nature lovers, while Percy Priest Lake offers opportunities for boating, fishing, and water sports. Bicentennial Capitol Mall State Park features expansive lawns, historical monuments, and a striking view of the Tennessee State Capitol.

As visitors navigate the city, they will encounter the warmth and friendliness of the locals, known for their genuine Southern hospitality. Nashville residents take pride in their city and are always willing to offer recommendations, share stories, and make visitors feel at home. The welcoming spirit of the city adds an extra layer of charm to the overall experience.

In this Nashville travel guide, we will delve deeper into the various aspects of the city, providing you with valuable information to make the most of your visit. We will explore the different neighborhoods, recommend must-visit attractions, highlight hidden gems, and provide insights into the best places to eat, shop, and experience the vibrant music scene. Whether you're planning a short getaway or an extended stay, this guide will serve as your companion to unlock the wonders of Music City USA.

So, get ready to embark on an unforgettable journey through the heart and soul of Nashville. Prepare to be enchanted by the music, enthralled by the history, tantalized by the flavors, and embraced by the warmth of this remarkable city. Let's dive in and discover all that Nashville has to offer, as we uncover the true essence of Music City USA.

Planning Your Nashville Adventure

Planning a trip to Nashville, the vibrant and culturally rich city of Music City USA, requires careful consideration and preparation to ensure a memorable and enjoyable experience. From deciding the best time to visit to arranging accommodations and creating an itinerary, this chapter will provide you with valuable insights and tips to plan your Nashville adventure.

Choosing the Best Time to Visit:

Nashville experiences a pleasant climate throughout the year, but each season offers a unique atmosphere. Spring and fall are particularly popular, with mild temperatures and blooming landscapes. Summers are warm and lively, perfect for outdoor activities and music festivals. Winter brings a quieter ambiance, with holiday decorations and opportunities to explore indoor attractions. Consider your preferences and interests when selecting the best time to visit Nashville.

Duration of Your Stay:

Determining the length of your stay is crucial for planning your activities and making the most of your time in Nashville. While a weekend trip can offer a taste of the city's highlights, a longer visit allows for deeper exploration of its various neighborhoods, attractions, and music venues. Plan your itinerary accordingly, ensuring a balance between must-see landmarks and leisurely experiences.

Booking Accommodations:

Nashville offers a diverse range of accommodations to suit different budgets and preferences. From luxury hotels and boutique inns to cozy bed and breakfasts and budget-friendly options, there are plenty of choices. Consider factors such as location, amenities, and proximity to attractions when selecting your accommodation. It is advisable to book in advance, especially during peak seasons and major events.

Transportation:

Decide on your preferred mode of transportation for getting to Nashville and getting around the city. Nashville International Airport (BNA) serves as the major gateway, with direct flights from numerous domestic and international destinations. Upon arrival, options for transportation within the city include renting a car, utilizing rideshare services, taking taxis, or utilizing the city's public transportation system. The choice depends on your comfort, convenience, and planned activities.

Researching Attractions and Landmarks:

Nashville is brimming with attractions and landmarks that cater to different interests. From music-related sites like the Country Music Hall of Fame and Museum, Grand Ole Opry, and Ryman Auditorium to historical landmarks like The Hermitage and Belle Meade Plantation, there is something for everyone. Research and create a list of the must-visit places based on your interests, allowing for a well-rounded Nashville experience.

Exploring Neighborhoods:

Nashville's neighborhoods each offer a distinct atmosphere and charm. Research the different neighborhoods, such as Downtown, East Nashville, Germantown, and 12 South, to understand their unique characteristics. Consider the dining options, shopping opportunities, nightlife scenes, and proximity to attractions when choosing the neighborhoods you wish to explore. It's also worthwhile to venture off the beaten path and discover hidden gems beyond the popular areas.

Live Music and Events:

Nashville's live music scene is unparalleled, and catching a live performance is a must-do. Research the schedules of famous venues like the Grand Ole Opry, Bluebird Cafe, and Station Inn to plan your attendance accordingly. Additionally, check the event calendars for festivals, concerts, and special events happening during your visit. These experiences provide a glimpse into the city's vibrant music culture.

Dining Experiences:

Nashville's culinary scene is diverse and enticing, offering a wide array of dining options. From traditional Southern cuisine to international flavors and innovative fusions, there is something to satisfy every palate. Research popular restaurants, food trucks, and local eateries to discover the culinary delights the city has to offer.

Don't forget to sample the iconic Nashville hot chicken, a local specialty.

Outdoor Activities:

Nashville is blessed with beautiful parks, gardens, and recreational areas. Research the outdoor activities available, such as hiking trails, kayaking on the Cumberland River, or picnicking in Centennial Park. Be sure to pack appropriate attire and gear based on the planned activities and the weather conditions during your visit.

Budgeting:

Determine your budget for the trip and allocate funds for accommodations, transportation, meals, attractions, and shopping. Consider the costs of popular attractions, parking fees, and any additional expenses you may incur. Researching admission prices, discounts, and package deals can help you make the most of your budget and avoid any unforeseen financial surprises.

Travel Insurance and Safety:

Consider purchasing travel insurance to protect yourself against any unexpected circumstances, such as trip cancellations or medical emergencies. Familiarize yourself with safety precautions and guidelines for the city, ensuring a safe and worry-free experience. Take note of emergency contact numbers and the location of the nearest medical facilities.

By considering these aspects and conducting thorough research, you can plan a well-organized and enjoyable Nashville adventure. Create an itinerary that reflects your interests, allowing you to immerse yourself in the vibrant music culture, explore the city's rich history, savor its culinary delights, and create lasting memories. Prepare to embark on an unforgettable journey through the heart and soul of Music City USA.

Getting Around: Transportation in Nashville

Navigating a new city can sometimes be a daunting task, but in Nashville, there are several transportation options available to make getting around a breeze. Whether you prefer the convenience of renting a car, the efficiency of public transportation, or the ease of rideshare services, this chapter will guide you through the various transportation options in Nashville.

Renting a Car:

Renting a car can provide flexibility and convenience, allowing you to explore Nashville and its surrounding areas at your own pace. Nashville has several car rental agencies located at the airport and throughout the city. It is advisable to book your car in advance, especially during peak travel seasons or major events. Keep in mind that parking can be limited and expensive in certain areas of downtown Nashville, so plan accordingly.

Public Transportation:

Nashville offers a public transportation system called the Nashville MTA (Metropolitan Transit Authority). The MTA operates buses that connect different neighborhoods and popular attractions throughout the city. The buses are equipped with amenities such as air conditioning and free Wi-Fi, making for a comfortable ride. You can purchase tickets directly from the driver or opt for a reloadable transit card for added convenience.

Familiarize yourself with the bus routes and schedules to plan your trips accordingly.

Music City Circuit:

A free bus service called the Music City Circuit is available in downtown Nashville. The Music City Circuit consists of three routes, making it easy to hop on and off at various attractions, hotels, and dining spots in the downtown area. This service is an excellent way to explore downtown Nashville without the hassle of driving or finding parking. The buses run at regular intervals, and route information can be found online or at designated bus stops.

Rideshare Services:

Rideshare services such as Uber and Lyft are popular and readily available in Nashville. These services provide a convenient and efficient way to get around the city, especially if you prefer not to drive or navigate public transportation. Simply download the app, request a ride, and wait for your driver to arrive. Rideshare services are commonly used by both visitors and locals, and they offer a convenient option for traveling to and from attractions, restaurants, and neighborhoods throughout Nashville.

Biking:

Nashville is a bike-friendly city with a growing network of bike lanes and trails. If you enjoy cycling, renting a bike can be a great way to explore the city while enjoying the fresh air and getting some exercise. Several bike rental shops offer a variety of bicycles, including traditional bikes, electric bikes, and even guided bike tours. Familiarize yourself with the city's bike infrastructure, including bike lanes and designated bike-friendly routes, to ensure a safe and enjoyable biking experience.

Walking:

Exploring Nashville on foot is a delightful way to soak in the city's vibrant atmosphere and discover hidden gems along the way. The downtown area is relatively compact, making it easy to navigate on foot. Many popular attractions, restaurants, and shops are within walking distance of each other, especially in the downtown and Broadway areas. However, be mindful of the weather, especially during the hot summer months, and wear comfortable shoes for walking longer distances.

Taxis:

Taxis are available in Nashville, although they are not as common as rideshare services. You can find taxis at designated taxi stands, hotels, or by calling a local taxi company. Taxis are a convenient option if you prefer the traditional method of transportation and if you require immediate service without the need for a smartphone or app. It is advisable to ask for an estimated fare or confirm the metered rate before beginning your journey.

Parking:

If you choose to rent a car or drive in

Nashville, it is essential to familiarize yourself with the parking options and regulations. Downtown Nashville has several parking garages and surface lots, but they can be expensive, especially during peak hours and events. Some hotels offer valet parking or have partnerships with nearby parking facilities, so it's worth checking with your accommodation. Additionally, be aware of street parking restrictions and meters to avoid parking violations.

Accessibility:

Nashville strives to be an accessible city for individuals with disabilities. Many transportation services, including buses and rideshare vehicles, are equipped to accommodate passengers with mobility needs. The Nashville MTA provides accessible buses with ramps and priority seating, and rideshare services offer options for wheelchair-accessible vehicles. If you require specific accommodations, it is recommended to contact the service provider or your accommodation in advance to ensure a seamless experience.

By familiarizing yourself with the transportation options available in Nashville, you can choose the method that suits your preferences and needs. Whether you opt for the convenience of renting a car, the affordability of public transportation, the ease of rideshare services, or the charm of walking and biking, Nashville offers a range of choices to explore the city and make the most of your visit. So, plan your transportation wisely and get ready to embark on an exciting Nashville adventure.

Where to Stay: Accommodation Options

When planning your trip to Nashville, one of the most important considerations is where to stay. Nashville offers a wide range of accommodation options to suit various budgets, preferences, and travel styles. Whether you're seeking luxury hotels, cozy bed and breakfasts, or budget-friendly accommodations, this chapter will guide you through the different areas and help you find the perfect place to stay during your Nashville adventure.

Downtown Nashville:

If you want to be at the heart of the action, staying in downtown Nashville is a great choice. This area is vibrant, with a lively atmosphere, numerous dining options, and easy access to iconic landmarks. You'll find a variety of accommodation options, including upscale hotels, boutique properties, and budget-friendly hotels. Many of the hotels in downtown Nashville offer stunning views of the city skyline and are within walking distance of popular attractions like the Country Music Hall of Fame and Museum, Ryman Auditorium, and the Honky Tonks on Lower Broadway.

The Gulch:

Located just southwest of downtown Nashville, The Gulch is a trendy and upscale neighborhood known for its chic boutiques, vibrant nightlife, and high-end dining options. The Gulch offers a range of boutique hotels and luxury accommodations that cater to those seeking a stylish and sophisticated stay. The area is also conveniently located near downtown Nashville, making it a popular choice for visitors who want easy access to both downtown attractions and The Gulch's upscale offerings.

East Nashville:

For a more bohemian and eclectic vibe, consider staying in East Nashville. This neighborhood is known for its artsy atmosphere, independent coffee shops, vintage stores, and a thriving local music scene. East Nashville offers a mix of accommodation options, including boutique hotels, bed and breakfasts, and vacation rentals. Staying in this neighborhood provides a unique opportunity to experience the creative side of Nashville and discover hidden gems that may be off the beaten path.

Midtown/Vanderbilt:

Located near Vanderbilt University, the Midtown area offers a blend of a college-town atmosphere and a lively entertainment scene. This neighborhood is home to various bars, restaurants, and music venues that cater to both locals and visitors. Midtown offers a range of accommodations, including hotels that cater to business travelers, as well as boutique properties and extended-stay options. Staying in Midtown provides a central location, with easy access to downtown Nashville and nearby attractions.

Opryland/Airport Area:

If you're attending a concert at the Grand Ole Opry or want to be near the Nashville International Airport (BNA), the Opryland/Airport area is a convenient choice. This neighborhood offers a mix of hotels, including well-known chains and mid-range options. The area is also close to popular attractions like the Opry Mills shopping center, the General Jackson Showboat, and the Gaylord Opryland Resort and Convention Center. Staying in this area provides easy access to the airport and attractions in the Opryland vicinity.

Music Row/Vanderbilt:

Music Row is the heart of Nashville's music industry, where you'll find recording studios, record labels, and the offices of music industry professionals. This area is located near Vanderbilt University, making it a popular choice for visitors attending events or visiting the campus. Accommodation options in Music Row/Vanderbilt range from mid-range hotels to extended-stay properties. Staying in this area allows you to immerse yourself in the music culture and history that Nashville is known for.

West End:

Located near Vanderbilt University and bordering Centennial Park, the West End area offers a mix of accommodation options, ranging from luxury hotels to budget-friendly choices. This neighborhood is popular with business travelers, families, and those looking for a more relaxed atmosphere. The proximity to Centennial Park allows visitors to enjoy outdoor activities and visit the Parthenon, a full-scale replica of the original structure in Athens. The West End area offers a peaceful retreat while still being close to downtown Nashville.

Suburban Areas:

If you prefer a quieter setting away from the hustle and bustle of downtown, Nashville's suburban areas provide a range of accommodation options. Areas like Brentwood, Franklin, and Bellevue offer a mix of hotels, extended-stay options, and vacation rentals. These suburban areas are ideal for those who want a more residential feel and are often preferred by families or travelers on extended stays. Although further from downtown, they offer a more relaxed ambiance and easy access to nearby attractions.

When choosing where to stay in Nashville, consider your preferences, budget, and the areas you plan to explore. Each neighborhood has its own unique charm and offers a different experience. It is also advisable to book your accommodations well in advance, especially during peak travel seasons or major events, to ensure availability. With Nashville's diverse range of accommodation options, you're sure to find the perfect place to stay and make your visit to Music City USA unforgettable.

Best Time to Visit Nashville

Nashville, also known as Music City USA, is a year-round destination with something to offer in every season. Each time of year in Nashville brings its own unique charm, weather conditions, and events. Whether you're a music lover, a food enthusiast, or a history buff, choosing the best time to visit Nashville will enhance your overall experience. In this chapter, we'll explore the different seasons and highlight the factors to consider when planning your trip to Music City.

Spring (March to May):

Spring is a popular time to visit Nashville, thanks to its mild temperatures and blooming landscapes. As winter gives way to spring, Nashville comes alive with vibrant colors and a sense of renewal. The city's numerous parks and gardens, such as Cheekwood Estate and Gardens and the Nashville Zoo at Grassmere, showcase beautiful spring blooms. This season is also known for outdoor events and festivals, including the Nashville Cherry Blossom Festival and the Tennessee Craft Fair. Spring is a great time to explore the city's outdoor attractions, enjoy outdoor dining, and catch live music performances at various venues.

Summer (June to August):

Summer in Nashville brings warmer temperatures and a lively atmosphere. This season is perfect for those who enjoy outdoor activities, music festivals, and events. The CMA Music Festival, held in June, attracts country music fans from around the world. The Nashville Shakespeare Festival, Bonnaroo Music and Arts Festival, and Live on the Green concert series are also popular summer events. With longer days, you'll have more time to explore the city's parks, take riverboat cruises on the Cumberland River, and enjoy outdoor dining at the many rooftop bars and patios. However, be prepared for higher temperatures and humidity during the summer months.

Fall (September to November):

Fall is arguably one of the best times to visit Nashville, as the weather cools down, and the city's foliage transforms into breathtaking shades of red, orange, and yellow. The fall season is ideal for outdoor activities such as hiking in nearby state parks or exploring the scenic Natchez Trace Parkway. Additionally, you can enjoy fall-themed events like the Tennessee State Fair, the Nashville Oktoberfest, and the Southern Festival of Books. The fall season also marks the start of football season, and Nashville's vibrant sports culture comes alive with Tennessee Titans NFL games and college football games at Vanderbilt University. Fall is a popular time for visitors, so be sure to book accommodations in advance.

Winter (December to February):

Winter in Nashville brings a quieter ambiance, with fewer tourists and a cozy atmosphere. Although temperatures can be chilly, the city still offers plenty of indoor attractions and activities to enjoy. The holiday season is particularly magical, with festive decorations, holiday markets, and the iconic Christmas lights at the Opryland Resort. Nashville's theaters and music venues host a variety of holiday concerts and performances, adding to the city's festive spirit. Winter is also an excellent time to explore the city's museums, such as the Country Music Hall of Fame and Museum or the Frist Art Museum. Additionally, hotel rates may be more affordable during this season, making it an attractive option for budget-conscious travelers.

Factors to Consider:

In addition to the seasons, several other factors should be considered when choosing the best time to visit Nashville:

Events and Festivals: Determine if there are specific events or festivals you'd like to attend during your visit. Nashville hosts a wide range of events throughout the year, and planning your trip around a particular festival can enhance your experience.

Budget: Consider the costs associated with your visit, including accommodation rates, airfare, and attractions. Traveling during the off-peak seasons or weekdays may offer more affordable options.

Personal Preferences: Think about your preferred weather conditions and activities. If you enjoy outdoor adventures, spring or fall may be the best fit. If you prefer indoor attractions or holiday festivities, winter might be the ideal choice.

Crowds: Take into account the level of tourism and crowds during different seasons. Spring and fall tend to be busier, while winter offers a quieter and more relaxed atmosphere.

Ultimately, the best time to visit Nashville depends on your personal interests, budget, and the type of experience you're seeking. Regardless of the season, Nashville's vibrant music scene, rich history, and warm hospitality await you. So, plan your trip accordingly, and get ready to immerse yourself in the dynamic energy of Music City USA.

Exploring Downtown Nashville

Downtown Nashville is the beating heart of Music City USA, offering a vibrant and energetic atmosphere that captures the essence of this renowned destination. From its iconic honky-tonks and historic landmarks to its vibrant arts scene and delectable dining options, downtown Nashville is a must-visit for anyone looking to immerse themselves in the city's rich culture and musical heritage. In this chapter, we will delve into the various attractions, experiences, and hidden gems that await you in downtown Nashville.

Lower Broadway and the Honky-Tonks:

Lower Broadway is the epicenter of Nashville's music scene, with its famous honky-tonks lining the streets. These lively establishments showcase live music performances day and night, offering an authentic and electrifying experience. From Tootsie's Orchid Lounge and Robert's Western World to Acme Feed & Seed and The Stage, you'll find an array of honky-tonks where you can listen to country, rock, and various other genres while enjoying a cold drink and the company of fellow music lovers.

Ryman Auditorium:

Known as the "Mother Church of Country Music," Ryman Auditorium is a Nashville icon and a must-visit for any music enthusiast. This historic venue has hosted legendary musicians and continues to be a premier concert destination. Take a guided backstage tour to learn about the Ryman's rich history and explore the exhibits that showcase its significance in the world of music. Attending a live performance at the Ryman is an unforgettable experience, as the venue's acoustics and intimate setting create a magical atmosphere.

The Country Music Hall of Fame and Museum:

Located on Fifth Avenue South, the Country Music Hall of Fame and Museum is a mecca for country music lovers. This iconic institution pays homage to the artists, songwriters, and industry professionals who have shaped the genre. Explore exhibits that showcase memorabilia, artifacts, and interactive displays, allowing you to dive deep into the history and evolution of country music. Don't miss the famous Hatch Show Print, a historic letterpress print shop located within the museum.

Printers Alley:

Step back in time and explore the historic Printers Alley, a narrow street filled with rich history and hidden gems. In its heyday, Printers Alley was home to numerous printing presses, publishing companies, and speakeasies. Today, it offers a unique blend of live music venues, bars, and restaurants. Immerse yourself in the storied past of Printers Alley as you wander through its vibrant alleyways, enjoy live performances, and savor the lively atmosphere.

The Johnny Cash Museum:

Dedicated to the life and legacy of the

legendary Johnny Cash, The Johnny Cash Museum is a must-visit for fans of the "Man in Black." Located on Third Avenue South, this museum showcases a vast collection of memorabilia, including stage costumes, handwritten lyrics, and personal artifacts. Immerse yourself in Cash's music, life, and impact on the world of country music as you explore the exhibits that pay homage to this iconic musician.

The Frist Art Museum:

Housed in a beautifully restored historic post office building, the Frist Art Museum is a premier art destination in downtown Nashville. The museum offers a diverse range of rotating exhibits, featuring local, national, and international artists across various mediums. Explore the thought-provoking and visually stunning exhibitions as you immerse yourself in the world of contemporary and classic art. The Frist Art Museum also hosts educational programs, lectures, and interactive experiences for visitors of all ages.

Nashville Symphony at the Schermerhorn Symphony Center:

If you're a fan of classical music, a visit to the Schermerhorn Symphony Center is a must. Home to the Nashville Symphony, this architectural masterpiece showcases world-class performances in a stunning venue. Experience the symphony's harmonious melodies as they fill the concert hall, and revel in the artistry of renowned musicians. Be sure to check the schedule and book tickets in advance to secure your spot for an unforgettable evening of musical excellence.

The Arcade:

Step into a piece of Nashville's history as you visit the Arcade, the city's oldest shopping center. Located between Fourth and Fifth Avenues, the Arcade is a beautiful and iconic structure that dates back to 1903. This indoor shopping mall features a charming array of specialty shops, boutiques, art galleries, and dining establishments. Stroll through its elegant corridors, admire the unique architecture, and discover one-of-a-kind treasures that make for perfect souvenirs.

Riverfront Park and the Cumberland River Pedestrian Bridge:

Enjoy Nashville's scenic beauty by taking a leisurely walk along the Cumberland River. Riverfront Park offers a tranquil escape from the bustling downtown area, with its sprawling green spaces, riverside views, and walking paths. Cross the Cumberland River Pedestrian Bridge, an iconic landmark that offers breathtaking panoramic views of the city skyline. This vantage point is particularly magical during sunset, as the city lights come alive, illuminating the skyline.

Dining and Nightlife:

Downtown Nashville is a culinary delight, with an abundance of dining options to suit every palate. From traditional Southern cuisine to international flavors and innovative culinary creations, you'll find it all in the city's vibrant food scene. Indulge in Nashville's famous hot chicken, savor mouthwatering barbecue, or explore the diverse array of cuisines offered in the city's numerous restaurants, cafes, and food halls. After dinner, immerse yourself in the lively nightlife scene, with numerous bars, rooftop lounges, and speakeasies offering live music, craft cocktails, and a spirited atmosphere.

As you explore downtown Nashville, allow yourself to be captivated by the city's rich musical heritage, cultural offerings, and lively ambiance. From the iconic honky-tonks and historic landmarks to the vibrant arts scene and delectable dining options, downtown Nashville is a vibrant and dynamic destination that guarantees an unforgettable experience. So, venture into the heart of Music City and let the rhythm of Nashville guide you through an extraordinary journey.

The Music Scene: Honky Tonks and Live Music Venues

When it comes to music, Nashville is an unrivaled destination. As the birthplace of country music and home to legendary recording studios, this city pulsates with a vibrant music scene that has captivated audiences for decades. From the iconic honky-tonks on Lower Broadway to the intimate live music venues scattered throughout the city, Nashville offers an unparalleled experience for music lovers. In this chapter, we will explore the honky-tonks, live music venues, and the rich history that defines Nashville's music scene.

Honky-Tonks on Lower Broadway:

Lower Broadway is the beating heart of Nashville's music scene, with its iconic honky-tonks lining the street. These lively establishments, such as Tootsie's Orchid Lounge, Robert's Western World, and Legends Corner, have become synonymous with Nashville's music culture. As you wander down Lower Broadway, you'll be greeted by the sounds of live music pouring out from each honky-tonk, inviting you to step inside and experience the electrifying performances. From classic country tunes to rock, blues, and everything in between, the honky-tonks offer a diverse range of music genres that cater to all tastes.

The Bluebird Cafe:

Located in a nondescript strip mall in Green Hills, the Bluebird Cafe holds a special place in Nashville's music scene. This intimate venue has gained international recognition as a premier listening room, known for showcasing singer-songwriters in an intimate and acoustic setting. Many renowned artists, including Taylor Swift, Garth Brooks, and Kathy Mattea, began their careers by performing at the Bluebird Cafe. The venue's small size and unassuming ambiance create an intimate and personal experience, allowing you to connect deeply with the music and stories shared on stage.

Ryman Auditorium:

No discussion of Nashville's music scene would be complete without mentioning the historic Ryman Auditorium. Known as the "Mother Church of Country Music," this legendary venue has hosted countless iconic musicians and has played a pivotal role in shaping the city's musical heritage. Originally built as a tabernacle in 1892, the Ryman Auditorium became the home of the Grand Ole Opry from 1943 to 1974. Today, it continues to host concerts, showcasing a wide array of music genres and providing an exceptional live music experience. Attending a show at the Ryman is a must for any music enthusiast, as the venue's acoustics and rich history create an unparalleled atmosphere.

Listening Rooms:

Nashville is known for its unique listening

rooms, where the focus is solely on the music. These intimate venues provide an up-close and personal experience, allowing you to truly appreciate the talent and artistry of the performers. The Listening Room Cafe, 3rd & Lindsley, and City Winery are among the notable listening rooms in Nashville. Whether you're a fan of country, Americana, folk, or any other genre, these venues offer a diverse range of performances that will captivate you with their authenticity and raw talent.

Grand Ole Opry:

No visit to Nashville would be complete without experiencing the Grand Ole Opry. As the longest-running live radio show in history, the Grand Ole Opry has been showcasing the best of country music since 1925. Held at various venues throughout the years, including the Ryman Auditorium and the Grand Ole Opry House, this iconic show continues to attract both established and emerging artists. Attending an Opry performance allows you to witness the rich tradition and storied legacy of country music, with its signature mix of classic hits and contemporary sounds.

The Station Inn:

For bluegrass and traditional country music enthusiasts, The Station Inn is a hidden gem. Tucked away in the Gulch neighborhood, this intimate venue has been hosting bluegrass performances since 1974. Known for its relaxed atmosphere and exceptional talent, The Station Inn attracts both local musicians and renowned artists. Grab a seat, order a cold drink, and let the soulful sounds of banjos, fiddles, and mandolins transport you to the heart of Appalachia.

Exit/In:

Exit/In is a historic live music venue located near Vanderbilt University. Since its opening in 1971, this venue has hosted countless rock, punk, and alternative acts, making it a staple of Nashville's live music scene. Exit/In has a gritty and energetic ambiance that perfectly complements its lineup of local and touring bands. If you're in the mood for a high-energy concert experience, be sure to check the schedule and catch a show at Exit/In.

Local Bars and Neighborhood Venues:

Beyond the famous honky-tonks and renowned venues, Nashville is home to numerous bars and neighborhood venues that offer exceptional live music experiences. In East Nashville, you'll find The 5 Spot, a neighborhood dive bar that hosts a variety of music genres, including soul, funk, and indie rock. In Midtown, you can enjoy live music at Winners Bar & Grill or Losers Bar & Grill, which are popular with both locals and visitors. These smaller, more intimate venues often showcase up-and-coming artists and provide an opportunity to discover the next big music sensation.

Nashville's music scene is a captivating

tapestry of genres, styles, and stories that continue to shape the city's cultural fabric. Whether you're exploring the lively honky-tonks on Lower Broadway, enjoying an intimate performance at the Bluebird Cafe, or attending a show at the iconic Ryman Auditorium, each experience offers a unique glimpse into the soul of Music City. So, immerse yourself in the vibrant rhythm and rich history of Nashville's music scene, and let the melodies and lyrics weave their magic during your visit to this extraordinary destination.

Nashville's Historic Landmarks and Museums

Nashville, the capital of Tennessee, is a city steeped in history and cultural significance. From its role in the Civil War to its prominence in the music industry, Nashville boasts a rich heritage that is showcased through its historic landmarks and museums. In this chapter, we will explore some of the must-visit historic sites and museums that offer a glimpse into the city's past and its contributions to music, art, and the nation's history.

The Parthenon:

Located in Centennial Park, the Parthenon is a full-scale replica of the original Parthenon in Athens, Greece. Built in 1897 as part of the Tennessee Centennial Exposition, this architectural masterpiece has since become one of Nashville's most iconic landmarks. Today, the Parthenon houses an art gallery that features a permanent collection of American art, as well as rotating exhibitions. Explore the stunning architecture, admire the statue of Athena Parthenos, and immerse yourself in the classical beauty of this unique landmark.

The Hermitage:

Step back in time and visit The Hermitage, the former home of President Andrew Jackson. Located just east of downtown Nashville, this historic site offers a glimpse into the life and legacy of the seventh president of the United States. Take a guided tour of the mansion, stroll through the beautiful gardens, and explore the museum exhibits that shed light on Jackson's impact on American history. The Hermitage also hosts special events and educational programs that provide a deeper understanding of this influential figure and the era in which he lived.

Belle Meade Plantation:

Experience the grandeur of the antebellum South at Belle Meade Plantation, a historic estate that dates back to the 19th century. Located in the upscale Belle Meade neighborhood, this Greek Revival mansion offers guided tours that delve into the history of the Harding and Jackson families who owned the plantation. Learn about the thoroughbred horse industry that thrived on the property and its impact on the region. The plantation also hosts wine tastings, showcasing the legacy of winemaking that began at Belle Meade in the 1800s.

Fort Negley:

Discover the Civil War history of Nashville at Fort Negley, a Union fortification that played a significant role during the war. Situated on St. Cloud Hill, Fort Negley offers panoramic views of the city skyline and provides insights into the city's wartime past. Explore the reconstructed fort, visit the interpretive center to learn about the fort's construction and significance, and stroll through the surrounding park to appreciate the natural beauty and tranquility of the site. Fort Negley serves as a testament to Nashville's history and the resilience of its inhabitants during a tumultuous period.

The Tennessee State Capitol:

Perched atop Capitol Hill, the Tennessee State Capitol is a stunning example of Greek Revival architecture. This historic landmark served as the home of Tennessee's government since its completion in 1859. Take a guided tour to explore the building's grand interiors, including the House and Senate chambers, and learn about the state's legislative history. The Capitol grounds also feature statues, memorials, and beautiful landscaping, providing a peaceful setting to reflect on the state's rich heritage and democratic institutions.

The Country Music Hall of Fame and Museum:

Dedicated to preserving and celebrating the history of country music, the Country Music Hall of Fame and Museum is a must-visit for music enthusiasts. Located in downtown Nashville, this iconic institution showcases the lives and legacies of country music's greatest artists, songwriters, and industry professionals. Explore the exhibits that feature memorabilia, artifacts, interactive displays, and multimedia presentations, allowing you to dive deep into the history and evolution of this beloved genre. The museum also hosts live performances, educational programs, and special events that offer a comprehensive experience for visitors of all ages.

The Johnny Cash Museum:

Pay homage to the legendary "Man in Black" at The Johnny Cash Museum. Located in downtown Nashville, this museum is dedicated to preserving the life and legacy of Johnny Cash, one of the most influential musicians in the history of country and rock music. Immerse yourself in Cash's music, career, and impact on popular culture as you explore the exhibits that feature personal artifacts, stage costumes, handwritten lyrics, and interactive displays. The museum provides a comprehensive look at the life of an iconic artist and his enduring impact on the music industry.

The Frist Art Museum:

Housed in a beautifully restored historic post office building, the Frist Art Museum is a premier art destination in Nashville. This museum showcases a diverse range of rotating exhibits, featuring local, national, and international artists across various mediums. Explore thought-provoking and visually stunning exhibitions that span from classic to contemporary art, photography, sculpture, and more. The Frist Art Museum also hosts educational programs, lectures, and interactive experiences, making it a dynamic cultural hub in the heart of downtown Nashville.

Nashville's historic landmarks and museums offer a tapestry of stories and experiences that showcase the city's rich history, artistic achievements, and cultural contributions. Whether you're exploring the iconic Parthenon, delving into the musical legacies at the Country Music Hall of Fame and Museum, or immersing yourself in the art world at the Frist Art Museum, each visit will deepen your understanding and appreciation of Nashville's vibrant heritage. So, embark on a journey through time and creativity as you explore the historic landmarks and museums that define Music City USA.

Discovering Nashville's Neighborhoods

Nashville is a city of vibrant neighborhoods, each with its own distinct character, charm, and attractions. From the historic streets of Germantown to the trendy boutiques of East Nashville, the city's neighborhoods offer a rich tapestry of culture, history, and local flavor. In this chapter, we will take a tour of some of Nashville's most notable neighborhoods, highlighting their unique offerings and must-visit destinations.

Downtown:

As the bustling heart of the city, downtown Nashville is a hub of activity, entertainment, and iconic landmarks. The area is known for its lively honky-tonks on Lower Broadway, where live music spills onto the streets day and night. In addition to the honky-tonks, downtown is home to major attractions such as the Country Music Hall of Fame and Museum, the Ryman Auditorium, and the Johnny Cash Museum. Downtown also offers a variety of dining options, from trendy restaurants to classic Southern cuisine, making it a perfect starting point for exploring the city.

Germantown:

Nashville's historic Germantown neighborhood is a charming district that boasts beautifully restored Victorian homes, trendy restaurants, and boutique shops. Take a leisurely stroll along the tree-lined streets and admire the architectural beauty of the neighborhood. Visit the

Bicentennial Capitol Mall State Park, which showcases Tennessee's history and features monuments and memorials. Enjoy a meal at one of the neighborhood's renowned restaurants, offering a diverse range of cuisines, including farm-to-table options and international flavors.

East Nashville:

East Nashville has become one of the city's trendiest and most vibrant neighborhoods. Known for its bohemian spirit and artistic atmosphere, East Nashville is a haven for musicians, artists, and creatives. Explore the quirky boutiques, art galleries, and vintage stores that line the streets of Five Points. Indulge in the neighborhood's thriving food scene, with a variety of farm-to-table restaurants, gastropubs, and ethnic eateries. East Nashville is also home to the renowned Shelby Bottoms Nature Center and Park, offering hiking and biking trails, as well as scenic views of the Cumberland River.

The Gulch:

Situated just south of downtown, The Gulch is a dynamic and upscale neighborhood known for its trendy restaurants, boutique shopping, and modern high-rise buildings. This former industrial area has been transformed into a vibrant destination with a mix of upscale residential complexes, hip hotels, and trendy shops. Enjoy a meal at one of the neighborhood's highly acclaimed restaurants, or head to one of the rooftop bars to enjoy panoramic views of the city skyline. The Gulch is also home to unique shops and boutiques, offering fashion, home decor, and artisanal goods.

12 South:

12 South is a lively and pedestrian-friendly neighborhood that offers a mix of trendy boutiques, eateries, and local charm. This vibrant district is known for its vibrant street art, music venues, and eclectic shops. Explore the vintage stores, artisanal bakeries, and specialty shops that line 12th Avenue South. Don't miss a visit to Sevier Park, where you can relax on the lawn, enjoy a picnic, or attend one of the neighborhood's many festivals and events. 12 South is a perfect neighborhood for a leisurely afternoon of shopping, dining, and soaking in the local atmosphere.

Hillsboro Village:

Located near Vanderbilt University, Hillsboro Village is a quaint and walkable neighborhood that exudes a youthful energy. This bustling district offers a mix of independent shops, locally owned restaurants, and cozy cafes. Browse the unique boutiques, catch a movie at the historic Belcourt Theatre, or indulge in a sweet treat from one of the neighborhood's charming bakeries. Hillsboro Village is a popular spot for both locals and visitors, thanks to its vibrant atmosphere and its proximity to the vibrant college community.

Sylvan Park:

Nestled just west of downtown, Sylvan Park is a residential neighborhood known for its quiet streets, historic homes, and family-friendly atmosphere. This charming district offers a mix of local restaurants, coffee shops, and neighborhood bars. Enjoy a leisurely walk along the tree-lined streets and explore McCabe Park, which features a public golf course, walking trails, and a community center. Sylvan Park's laid-back ambiance and local charm make it a perfect neighborhood to unwind and experience a slice of Nashville's residential life.

Edgehill Village:

Situated near Music Row, Edgehill Village is a vibrant and evolving neighborhood that blends history with a modern sensibility. The area features a mix of renovated bungalows, contemporary homes, and hip businesses. Explore the unique shops, art galleries, and eateries that call Edgehill Village home. The neighborhood is also known for its diverse culinary scene, with restaurants offering global flavors and creative fusion dishes. Enjoy a cup of coffee at a local cafe, or catch a live performance at one of the intimate music venues in the area.

Nashville's neighborhoods offer a diverse range of experiences, allowing visitors to immerse themselves in the city's local culture, history, and vibrant atmosphere. From the lively honky-tonks of downtown to the artistic energy of East Nashville, each neighborhood has its own unique character and attractions to explore. So, venture beyond the downtown area and discover the hidden gems that await you in Nashville's diverse and dynamic neighborhoods.

Family-Friendly Activities in Nashville

Nashville is not just a destination for music lovers and food enthusiasts—it's also a city that offers a plethora of family-friendly activities and attractions. From interactive museums to outdoor adventures, there are plenty of opportunities for families to create lasting memories in Music City. In this chapter, we will explore some of the top family-friendly activities in Nashville, ensuring that your visit is enjoyable for every member of the family.

Adventure Science Center:

The Adventure Science Center is a fantastic destination for families with children of all ages. This interactive museum features hands-on exhibits that cover a wide range of scientific topics, from astronomy and physics to biology and robotics. Kids can explore the wonders of space in the planetarium, conduct experiments in the science lab, and engage in educational programs and demonstrations. With its engaging exhibits and immersive experiences, the Adventure Science Center provides an entertaining and educational outing for the whole family.

Nashville Zoo at Grassmere:

Located on 200 acres of beautiful grounds, the Nashville Zoo at Grassmere is home to over 3,000 animals from around the world. Families can embark on a safari adventure as they explore the zoo's various exhibits, including the African

Savannah, the Jungle Gym playground, and the Bamboo Trail. Don't miss the opportunity to feed the lorikeets in the colorful aviary or watch the playful antics of the red pandas. The Nashville Zoo offers a variety of educational programs, animal encounters, and events that cater to children of all ages.

Adventure Park at Nashville:

For families seeking outdoor thrills, the Adventure Park at Nashville is a perfect destination. This aerial adventure park features zip lines, treetop obstacle courses, and climbing challenges suitable for all skill levels. Strap on a harness and navigate through a series of suspended bridges, rope swings, and zip lines while enjoying breathtaking views of the surrounding forest. The Adventure Park at Nashville offers a range of courses designed specifically for children, ensuring a fun and safe experience for the whole family.

Lane Motor Museum:

Car enthusiasts of all ages will appreciate a visit to the Lane Motor Museum, a unique institution dedicated to showcasing rare and unusual vehicles from around the world. With over 500 cars and motorcycles on display, the museum offers a fascinating journey through the history of automotive design and innovation. Children will be captivated by the collection of microcars, amphibious vehicles, and vintage automobiles. The museum also hosts interactive exhibits and workshops that allow kids to learn about the mechanics and engineering behind these fascinating machines.

Nashville Children's Theatre:

Immerse your family in the world of theater at the Nashville Children's Theatre. As the oldest professional children's theater company in the country, this institution offers a range of captivating performances specifically designed for young audiences. From classic tales to original productions, the Nashville Children's Theatre provides an opportunity for children to experience the magic of live theater and storytelling. Check the schedule for upcoming shows and engage your family in a memorable theatrical experience.

Cumberland Park:

Situated along the Cumberland River, Cumberland Park is a waterfront park that offers a variety of family-friendly activities. Children can splash and play in the water features of the splash pad, climb the colorful play structures, and explore the rock climbing wall. The park also features walking trails, picnic areas, and beautiful views of the Nashville skyline. Pack a picnic, enjoy a leisurely stroll, or simply relax while the kids burn off energy in this engaging and scenic park.

The Nashville Public Library:

The Nashville Public Library is not just a place for books—it also offers a wealth of family-friendly activities and programs. From storytimes and puppet shows to arts and crafts workshops, the library provides a welcoming and enriching environment for children of all ages. Explore the children's section, which features a vast collection of books, educational resources, and interactive exhibits. The library also hosts special events, such as author visits and themed activities, that are sure to engage and entertain young minds.

Centennial Sportsplex:

If your family enjoys sports and outdoor activities, the Centennial Sportsplex is the perfect destination. This expansive facility offers a range of amenities, including ice skating rinks, swimming pools, and tennis courts. Whether you're a beginner or an experienced athlete, there are opportunities for everyone to participate in recreational sports and activities. Take an ice skating lesson, make a splash in the pool, or challenge each other to a friendly tennis match. The Centennial Sportsplex provides a fun and active environment for families to stay active and enjoy quality time together.

Nashville offers an abundance of family-friendly activities that cater to all interests and ages. From interactive museums and outdoor adventures to cultural experiences and entertainment venues, there is something for everyone in Music City. So, plan your itinerary accordingly, and get ready to create cherished memories with your family as you explore the diverse and exciting attractions that Nashville has to offer.

Outdoor Adventures in and around the City

While Nashville is known for its vibrant music scene and rich cultural heritage, it also offers a wealth of outdoor adventures for those seeking to explore the natural beauty of the region. From scenic parks and greenways to hiking trails and water activities, there are plenty of opportunities to enjoy the great outdoors in and around the city. In this chapter, we will delve into some of the top outdoor adventures that Nashville has to offer, ensuring that you make the most of your visit to Music City.

Percy Warner Park and Edwin Warner Park:

Located just west of downtown, Percy Warner Park and Edwin Warner Park collectively make up one of the largest urban park systems in the United States. These interconnected parks offer a variety of outdoor activities, including hiking, biking, horseback riding, and picnicking. Explore the miles of trails that wind through scenic woodlands, rolling hills, and peaceful meadows. Be sure to visit the iconic stone steps at Percy Warner Park, which provide a challenging but rewarding hike with panoramic views of the surrounding area.

Radnor Lake State Park:

Nestled in the heart of the city, Radnor Lake State Park offers a peaceful retreat from the hustle and bustle of urban life. The park features over six miles of trails that meander through tranquil forests and around the picturesque Radnor Lake.

Nature enthusiasts will appreciate the park's diverse wildlife, including waterfowl, deer, and various bird species. Take a leisurely hike, rent a kayak, or join a ranger-led educational program to discover the beauty and serenity of this natural oasis.

Harpeth River State Park:

For water enthusiasts and nature lovers, a visit to Harpeth River State Park is a must. Located just west of Nashville, this park offers a variety of water activities, including kayaking, canoeing, and fishing. Explore the meandering Harpeth River, which flows through a scenic gorge and past towering limestone bluffs. The park also features several hiking trails that showcase the natural beauty of the area. Be sure to visit the historic Montgomery Bell Tunnel, a man-made tunnel dating back to the 19th century, which adds a touch of history to your outdoor adventure.

Cheekwood Estate and Gardens:

Nestled on 55 acres of stunning gardens and woodland, Cheekwood Estate and Gardens is a paradise for nature lovers and art enthusiasts alike. Explore the meticulously manicured gardens, featuring a variety of flora, sculptures, and water features. Take a leisurely stroll along the woodland trails, which offer breathtaking views of the surrounding landscapes. Cheekwood also hosts art exhibits, educational programs, and seasonal events, making it a vibrant destination throughout the year.

Percy Priest Lake:

Located just east of Nashville, Percy Priest Lake is a popular destination for water-based activities. The lake offers opportunities for boating, fishing, swimming, and picnicking. Rent a pontoon boat, kayak, or paddleboard and explore the scenic coves and inlets of the lake. Fishing enthusiasts will appreciate the abundance of bass, crappie, and catfish in the waters. The lake's sandy beaches and designated swimming areas provide a refreshing respite during the summer months.

Bicentennial Capitol Mall State Park:

Situated near the Tennessee State Capitol, Bicentennial Capitol Mall State Park offers a unique blend of history, art, and outdoor recreation. Explore the park's expansive green spaces, which feature walking paths, fountains, and monuments that commemorate Tennessee's history. Be sure to visit the World War II Memorial and the Tennessee Amphitheater, which hosts live performances and cultural events. The park also offers panoramic views of the Nashville skyline, making it a picturesque spot for a leisurely stroll or a picnic.

Stones River Greenway:

For those who enjoy biking, walking, or jogging, the Stones River Greenway offers a scenic route along the Stones River and through various parks and green spaces. This paved trail system spans over ten miles and connects several neighborhoods and recreational areas in the

Nashville area. Enjoy the natural beauty of the river, pass through shaded forests, and discover hidden gems along the way, such as the historic Two Rivers Mansion. The Stones River Greenway provides a peaceful and enjoyable outdoor experience for the whole family.

Cumberland River Cruises:

Experience Nashville from a different perspective by embarking on a cruise along the Cumberland River. Several companies offer riverboat cruises that provide scenic views of the city's skyline, narrated tours, and even live entertainment. Enjoy a leisurely sightseeing cruise, a romantic dinner cruise, or a lively party cruise as you glide along the majestic river. The cruises offer a unique opportunity to relax, enjoy the scenery, and learn about the history and culture of Nashville.

Nashville's outdoor adventures offer a diverse range of activities that cater to all interests and ages. Whether you prefer hiking through scenic parks, exploring waterways, or simply enjoying the beauty of well-manicured gardens, there is something for everyone in Music City. So, lace up your hiking boots, pack your picnic basket, and get ready to immerse yourself in the natural wonders that surround Nashville.

Shopping in Music City: Unique Boutiques and Malls

Nashville is not just a haven for music enthusiasts—it's also a vibrant destination for shoppers seeking unique finds, trendy fashion, and local treasures. From stylish boutiques and artisanal shops to bustling malls and markets, the city offers a diverse shopping scene that caters to all tastes and budgets. In this chapter, we will explore some of the top shopping destinations in Nashville, ensuring that you have an unforgettable retail experience during your visit to Music City.

Hillsboro Village:

Located near Vanderbilt University, Hillsboro Village is a charming neighborhood known for its eclectic mix of boutiques, specialty shops, and local eateries. This pedestrian-friendly district offers a diverse range of shopping options, from clothing and accessories to home decor and handmade goods. Explore boutiques like Posh Boutique and Posh Home, which offer stylish fashion and unique home decor items. Don't miss the opportunity to browse the selection of records and vintage treasures at Grimey's New & Preloved Music. Hillsboro Village is the perfect destination for those seeking a blend of local charm and trendy finds.

12 South:

12 South is a trendy neighborhood known for its vibrant atmosphere, local boutiques, and

artisanal shops. Take a leisurely stroll along 12th Avenue South and explore the unique offerings of this popular shopping district. Immerse yourself in fashion-forward boutiques like Emerson Grace and Hero, which showcase curated collections of clothing, accessories, and jewelry. Discover the latest trends in home decor and gifts at White's Mercantile, a modern take on the general store concept. For a sweet treat, indulge in handcrafted chocolates and confections at Five Daughters Bakery. 12 South offers a delightful shopping experience that perfectly captures the spirit of Nashville's hip and trendy scene.

East Nashville:

East Nashville is a bohemian neighborhood that embraces creativity and individuality, reflected in its eclectic mix of independent boutiques and vintage shops. Explore the unique finds at shops like Goodbuy Girls, which specializes in vintage and curated clothing for men and women. Serendipity, a locally owned boutique, offers a wide range of stylish clothing, accessories, and home goods. For vinyl enthusiasts, The Groove is a must-visit record store that stocks a diverse selection of new and used records across various genres. East Nashville's vibrant shopping scene allows visitors to discover one-of-a-kind pieces and support local artisans.

Opry Mills:

For a comprehensive shopping experience, visit Opry Mills, one of the largest outlet malls in the Southeast. Located near the Grand Ole Opry, this expansive shopping destination features over 200 stores, including popular brands like Coach, Nike, and Gap. Whether you're searching for fashion, accessories, home decor, or electronics, Opry Mills offers a wide range of options at discounted prices. In addition to shopping, the mall also features entertainment options, such as a movie theater and a variety of dining establishments, making it a one-stop destination for retail therapy and family fun.

The Gulch:

The Gulch is a vibrant neighborhood that blends modern sophistication with local charm. This trendy district offers a mix of upscale boutiques, specialty shops, and art galleries. Explore the curated collections of contemporary fashion and accessories at boutiques like e.Allen and Two Old Hippies. Admire unique works of art at galleries like The Studio 208 and The Rymer Gallery, which showcase local and regional artists. The Gulch also features a variety of lifestyle stores, home decor shops, and beauty salons, ensuring that you find everything you need for a stylish and personalized shopping experience.

Marathon Village:

Located in a former car factory, Marathon Village is a historic complex that houses an array of local shops, studios, and artisanal workshops. Discover unique treasures and vintage finds at Antique Archaeology, the flagship store of the

American Pickers TV show. Explore local craftsmanship at Nelson's Green Brier Distillery, where you can sample and purchase Tennessee whiskey and spirits. Don't miss the opportunity to browse the handmade jewelry, clothing, and accessories at local boutiques like Corsair Artisan and Sugar Dive. Marathon Village offers a distinct shopping experience that celebrates Nashville's history and creativity.

Downtown Nashville:

While downtown Nashville is famous for its music venues and honky-tonks, it also offers a variety of shopping opportunities. Lower Broadway, in particular, is home to a mix of souvenir shops, boot stores, and western wear boutiques. Explore shops like Boot Country and Trail West for an extensive selection of boots, hats, and western apparel. For unique Nashville-themed gifts and souvenirs, visit shops like Nashville-themed gifts and souvenirs, visit shops like The Music City Shop and the Hatch Show Print store. Downtown Nashville provides a lively and bustling shopping experience that captures the spirit of Music City.

The Factory at Franklin:

Located just south of Nashville in Franklin, The Factory at Franklin is a unique shopping destination housed in a historic factory building. This vibrant complex features a mix of shops, galleries, and restaurants. Discover locally made goods, artisanal crafts, and boutique clothing at shops like Finnleys, Draper James, and White's Mercantile. The Factory also hosts regular events, including farmers markets, art shows, and live performances, providing a lively and engaging atmosphere for shoppers of all ages.

Nashville's shopping scene is as diverse and vibrant as its music culture. Whether you're in search of trendy fashion, unique souvenirs, or locally made goods, the city offers an array of shopping destinations that cater to all tastes. So, get ready to shop 'til you drop and explore the unique boutiques, bustling malls, and artisanal shops that make Music City a shopper's paradise.

Dining Experiences: Southern Cuisine and Beyond

Nashville is not only known for its vibrant music scene but also for its diverse and mouthwatering culinary offerings. From traditional Southern comfort food to innovative fusion dishes, the city boasts a thriving food scene that caters to all tastes and preferences. In this chapter, we will explore the dining experiences that await you in Music City, highlighting the iconic Southern cuisine as well as the exciting culinary influences from around the world.

Southern Comfort Food:

No visit to Nashville would be complete without indulging in the city's renowned Southern comfort food. From fried chicken and biscuits to macaroni and cheese, these classic dishes embody the warm and hearty flavors of the region. Head to Loveless Cafe, a Nashville institution famous for its country ham, homemade preserves, and mouthwatering biscuits. Another beloved spot is Hattie B's Hot Chicken, where you can savor Nashville's signature spicy fried chicken. For a taste of traditional meat-and-three, visit Arnold's Country Kitchen, which offers a daily rotating menu of Southern staples. Embrace the soulful flavors of the South and experience the comforting delights of Nashville's Southern cuisine.

Hot Chicken:

Hot chicken is a Nashville specialty that has

gained worldwide acclaim. This fiery and flavorful dish consists of deep-fried chicken coated in a blend of spices, typically served with pickles and white bread. Sample the city's iconic hot chicken at Prince's Hot Chicken Shack, the originator of this fiery delight. Choose your preferred level of spiciness, ranging from mild to extra hot, and prepare for a flavor explosion. Other notable hot chicken spots include Hattie B's Hot Chicken, Bolton's Spicy Chicken & Fish, and Party Fowl. Dive into the fiery world of hot chicken and discover why it has become a Nashville culinary phenomenon.

Barbecue:

Nashville's barbecue scene is rich and diverse, offering a variety of regional styles and flavors. From Memphis-style dry ribs to tangy Carolina pulled pork, barbecue lovers will find their taste buds satisfied in Music City. Head to Martin's Bar-B-Que Joint, known for its mouthwatering smoked meats and scratch-made sides. Enjoy a platter of slow-smoked ribs, brisket, or pulled pork, paired with classic Southern sides like collard greens and macaroni and cheese. For a taste of unique flavors, visit Peg Leg Porker, where you can sample award-winning Tennessee-style barbecue and indulge in their signature "Peg Leg" sandwich. Nashville's barbecue joints are a haven for meat lovers and offer a true taste of Southern culinary traditions.

Farm-to-Table Cuisine:

Nashville embraces the farm-to-table movement, with many restaurants prioritizing locally sourced ingredients and seasonal produce. Experience the freshness and flavors of locally grown ingredients at restaurants like Rolf and Daughters, where the menu showcases modern American cuisine with a focus on regional ingredients. City House, located in the historic Germantown neighborhood, offers an Italian-inspired menu featuring locally sourced meats and produce. Another notable farm-to-table destination is The Catbird Seat, a chef-driven restaurant where diners can experience a unique tasting menu crafted from locally sourced ingredients. Indulge in the flavors of the season and support local farmers as you savor Nashville's farm-to-table offerings.

International Flavors:

Nashville's food scene goes beyond Southern cuisine, offering a diverse range of international flavors and culinary influences. Explore the vibrant neighborhoods of Nashville and discover a variety of international dining options. Visit Little Octopus, a Latin-American inspired eatery that offers a fresh and inventive menu of ceviches, tacos, and tropical cocktails. Thai Esane is a popular spot for authentic Thai cuisine, serving dishes bursting with bold flavors and aromatic spices. For sushi lovers, Samurai Sushi offers an extensive selection of traditional Japanese rolls and sashimi. Nashville's international culinary scene reflects the city's multicultural fabric and provides a delightful array of global flavors.

Craft Breweries:

In recent years, Nashville has emerged as a hub for craft breweries, offering an impressive selection of locally brewed beers. Enjoy a pint of handcrafted brews at breweries like Yazoo Brewing Company, known for its wide range of beers, from hoppy IPAs to rich stouts. Bearded Iris Brewing specializes in hop-forward beers and hazy IPAs, while TailGate Brewery offers a family-friendly atmosphere with an expansive selection of beers and outdoor games. Experience the art of craft brewing and savor the distinct flavors of Nashville's local brews.

Food Halls:

For those seeking a diverse culinary experience, Nashville's food halls are a perfect destination. These dynamic spaces house multiple vendors, offering a variety of cuisines and flavors under one roof. The Assembly Food Hall features a collection of food stalls serving everything from wood-fired pizza to sushi and gourmet sandwiches. Visit the Nashville Farmer's Market, where you can explore a wide selection of local produce, artisanal goods, and international food stalls. The food halls provide a vibrant and communal dining experience, allowing you to sample an array of flavors in one convenient location.

Desserts and Sweet Treats:

Finish off your culinary journey in Nashville with delectable desserts and sweet treats. Visit Goo

Goo Cluster, the birthplace of the iconic Southern candy bar, and indulge in a variety of chocolatey creations. For homemade ice cream, head to Jeni's Splendid Ice Creams, known for its unique and innovative flavors made with high-quality ingredients. Don't miss the opportunity to savor the famous Southern pies at The Pie Wagon, a local favorite serving up classic flavors like pecan and chess pie. Treat yourself to the sweet delights of Music City and satisfy your sweet tooth with Nashville's delectable desserts.

Nashville's dining scene is a reflection of the city's vibrant culture and culinary creativity. Whether you're craving classic Southern comfort food, fiery hot chicken, international flavors, or artisanal delights, the city offers a wide range of dining experiences to suit every palate. So, embark on a culinary adventure in Music City and savor the diverse flavors and culinary traditions that make Nashville a true food lover's paradise.

Nashville's Craft Beer and Distillery Scene

When it comes to craft beer and spirits, Nashville has established itself as a prominent player in the craft beverage industry. With a growing number of breweries and distilleries, the city offers a diverse range of locally brewed beers, artisanal spirits, and unique tasting experiences. In this chapter, we will explore Nashville's craft beer and distillery scene, highlighting some of the must-visit establishments that will delight beer enthusiasts and spirit connoisseurs alike.

Yazoo Brewing Company:

Founded in 2003, Yazoo Brewing Company is one of Nashville's oldest and most respected craft breweries. Located in the Gulch neighborhood, Yazoo is known for its wide range of high-quality beers that showcase a variety of styles and flavors. Take a brewery tour to learn about the brewing process and the history of Yazoo, and then indulge in a tasting session to sample their diverse beer lineup. From hoppy IPAs and robust stouts to Belgian-inspired ales, Yazoo Brewing Company offers a beer for every palate.

Jackalope Brewing Company:

Jackalope Brewing Company is another local favorite that has made a name for itself in Nashville's craft beer scene. Founded in 2011, Jackalope is known for its creative and innovative brews. Their flagship beer, the Thunder Ann American Pale Ale, is a favorite among locals and visitors alike. Jackalope's taproom provides a cozy and inviting atmosphere to enjoy their beers, and they often host special events and food truck rallies. Don't miss the opportunity to try their seasonal and limited-release offerings for a true taste of their craft brewing prowess.

Bearded Iris Brewing:

Bearded Iris Brewing has gained widespread acclaim for its exceptional IPAs and hazy New England-style beers. Situated in East Nashville, Bearded Iris is known for its commitment to brewing hop-forward, flavorful, and aromatic beers. Their taproom offers a laid-back and welcoming environment where beer enthusiasts can sample a variety of rotating beers on tap. From juicy IPAs bursting with tropical hop flavors to rich and smooth stouts, Bearded Iris Brewing is a must-visit destination for those seeking top-notch craft beer.

Corsair Distillery:

Corsair Distillery is a true pioneer in Nashville's craft distillery scene, specializing in unique and experimental spirits. Founded in 2008, Corsair is known for its adventurous approach to distilling, producing a wide range of spirits, including whiskey, gin, rum, and vodka. Take a distillery tour to learn about the distilling process and the innovative techniques employed by Corsair. Enjoy a tasting flight of their award-winning spirits, which often include intriguing flavors and unconventional ingredients. Corsair's distillery locations in Marathon Village and Wedgewood-Houston offer a distinct and immersive experience for spirits enthusiasts.

Nelson's Green Brier Distillery:

Step back in time and experience the rich history of Nashville's distilling heritage at Nelson's Green Brier Distillery. Founded in the 1800s and revived by the original family's descendants, this historic distillery produces premium whiskey using traditional methods. Take a guided tour of the distillery to learn about the history of the Green Brier brand and the distillation process. Sample their signature Belle Meade Bourbon and other small-batch whiskeys, and gain an appreciation for the craftsmanship and attention to detail that goes into every bottle.

Tennessee Brew Works:

Tennessee Brew Works is a brewery and taproom located in downtown Nashville, offering a selection of handcrafted beers that celebrate the flavors and traditions of Tennessee. Their brewmaster takes inspiration from local ingredients, incorporating flavors like sweet potatoes, honey, and local coffee into their unique brews. Enjoy a flight of their beers in the taproom or grab a pint of their signature Southern Wit, Country Roots, or State Park Blonde. Tennessee Brew Works also hosts events and live music, creating a vibrant and social atmosphere for beer enthusiasts.

Nelson's Green Brier Brewery:

Nelson's Green Brier Brewery, an extension of the Green Brier Distillery, focuses on crafting small-batch, high-quality beers with a nod to Nashville's brewing history. Situated in Marathon Village, the brewery offers a cozy taproom where visitors can sample a rotating selection of beers brewed on-site. From classic styles like pale ales and IPAs to experimental and seasonal brews, Nelson's Green Brier Brewery showcases the diversity of Nashville's craft beer scene.

Diskin Cider:

For cider lovers, Diskin Cider is a must-visit destination in Nashville. This craft cidery specializes in producing high-quality, small-batch ciders using traditional methods and locally sourced ingredients. Diskin Cider offers a variety of flavors, from crisp and dry ciders to those infused with fruits and spices. Visit their taproom to enjoy a flight of ciders, learn about the cider-making process, and experience the unique flavors of their offerings.

Nashville's craft beer and distillery scene is a testament to the city's passion for quality craftsmanship and innovation. Whether you're a beer enthusiast or a spirits connoisseur, the breweries and distilleries in Music City offer a rich tapestry of flavors and experiences. So, embark on a tasting journey, savor the distinctive flavors, and raise a glass to Nashville's thriving craft beer and distillery scene.

Exploring Nashville's Parks and Green Spaces

Nashville, also known as the "Athens of the South," is not only renowned for its vibrant music scene but also for its abundant parks and green spaces. The city boasts a wealth of natural beauty, from scenic parks and serene lakes to expansive greenways and botanical gardens. In this chapter, we will explore some of the top parks and green spaces in Nashville, inviting you to immerse yourself in the tranquility and natural splendor that Music City has to offer.

Centennial Park:

Centennial Park, located near Vanderbilt University, is one of Nashville's most iconic and beloved parks. Spanning 132 acres, the park is home to the famous full-scale replica of the Parthenon, which stands as a testament to Nashville's nickname. Take a leisurely stroll around the park's walking paths, enjoy a picnic in the open green spaces, or relax by the tranquil Lake Watauga. Centennial Park also hosts various events and festivals throughout the year, including outdoor concerts and art shows. It is a true urban oasis that offers a blend of history, culture, and natural beauty.

Radnor Lake State Park:

For a tranquil escape from the bustling city, Radnor Lake State Park is a must-visit destination. Located just minutes from downtown Nashville, this 1,332-acre park offers pristine woodlands, peaceful trails, and a picturesque lake. Take a leisurely hike along the park's well-maintained trails, which wind through lush forests and provide breathtaking views of the lake. Wildlife enthusiasts will appreciate the park's diverse ecosystem, home to numerous bird species, turtles, deer, and more. Radnor Lake State Park offers a serene retreat for those seeking solace in nature.

Percy Warner Park and Edwin Warner Park:

Percy Warner Park and Edwin Warner Park collectively make up one of the largest urban park systems in the United States. These interconnected parks offer over 3,100 acres of rolling hills, wooded areas, and scenic trails. Percy Warner Park is known for its iconic stone steps, which provide a challenging but rewarding hiking experience and offer panoramic views of the surrounding area. Edwin Warner Park features a variety of recreational activities, including picnic areas, playgrounds, and sports fields. Together, these parks provide ample opportunities for hiking, biking, picnicking, and wildlife spotting.

Shelby Bottoms Nature Center and Greenway:

Shelby Bottoms Nature Center and Greenway is a 960-acre park located along the Cumberland River. This expansive green space offers a variety of outdoor activities, including walking trails, biking paths, and fishing spots. Explore the park's diverse ecosystems, which include wetlands, forests, and open meadows, providing habitats for a wide range of wildlife. The nature center offers educational exhibits and programs that highlight the park's natural history and environmental importance. Whether you're a nature enthusiast, a fitness enthusiast, or simply looking for a peaceful retreat, Shelby Bottoms Nature Center and Greenway has something for everyone.

Bicentennial Capitol Mall State Park:

Situated in the heart of downtown Nashville, Bicentennial Capitol Mall State Park is not your typical park. It is a living tribute to Tennessee's history and serves as an outdoor museum and civic gathering space. Stroll along the park's 19-acre grounds and discover various monuments, including the Tennessee Amphitheater, the World War II Memorial, and the Court of 3 Stars. Learn about Tennessee's rich heritage through the park's informative displays and historical markers. Bicentennial Capitol Mall State Park also features beautiful landscaping, fountains, and walking paths, making it a serene spot for reflection and relaxation in the heart of the city.

Cumberland Park:

Located along the Cumberland River, Cumberland Park offers a unique blend of natural beauty and interactive play spaces. The park's unique design incorporates water features, climbing structures, and a sand play area, creating a dynamic and engaging environment for families and children. Take a leisurely walk along the riverfront, enjoy a picnic on the grassy lawns, or cool off in the water fountains during the hot summer months. Cumberland Park is a perfect destination for families and individuals seeking outdoor fun and relaxation.

Cheekwood Estate and Gardens:

Situated on 55 acres of beautifully landscaped gardens and woodlands, Cheekwood Estate and Gardens is a true gem in Nashville. This historic estate features stunning botanical gardens, sculptures, and art exhibits. Explore the themed gardens, such as the Japanese Garden and the Color Garden, which showcase a diverse array of plant species and offer a peaceful retreat for visitors. Cheekwood also hosts seasonal events and exhibitions, including the popular "Cheekwood in Bloom" festival during spring, when the gardens come alive with vibrant colors and fragrances. Immerse yourself in the natural beauty and artistic wonders of Cheekwood Estate and Gardens.

Warner Parks Nature Center:

Located within Percy Warner Park, the Warner Parks Nature Center is an educational and recreational hub that offers a range of programs and activities for visitors of all ages. The center provides nature exhibits, interactive displays, and guided hikes that allow visitors to learn about the local flora, fauna, and natural history of the parks. Attend a nature program, join a guided hike, or simply explore the center's trails to deepen your understanding and appreciation of the natural wonders that surround Nashville.

Nashville's parks and green spaces provide a

sanctuary of tranquility and natural beauty amidst the city's vibrant energy. Whether you're seeking a peaceful stroll, an outdoor adventure, or a family outing, Music City offers a diverse range of options to reconnect with nature. So, lace up your walking shoes, pack a picnic, and embark on a journey to explore the parks and green spaces that make Nashville a haven for outdoor enthusiasts.

Day Trips from Nashville: Nearby Attractions

While Nashville has plenty to offer, sometimes it's nice to venture beyond the city and explore the surrounding areas. Fortunately, there are numerous attractions within a short drive from Nashville that make for excellent day trips. From historic towns and natural wonders to cultural landmarks and outdoor adventures, these nearby destinations offer a diverse range of experiences for travelers. In this chapter, we will take a closer look at some of the top day trip options from Nashville, ensuring that you make the most of your time in the region.

Franklin:

Located just 20 miles south of Nashville, Franklin is a charming historic town that offers a glimpse into the past. Take a leisurely stroll along Main Street, lined with preserved 19th-century buildings housing boutiques, antique shops, and art galleries. Visit the Carnton historic plantation and museum to learn about the area's Civil War history, or explore the Lotz House, an antebellum home that serves as a museum showcasing period furniture and artifacts. Franklin also boasts a vibrant dining scene, with a variety of restaurants offering Southern cuisine, farm-to-table delights, and international flavors. Immerse yourself in the rich history and warm hospitality of Franklin on a day trip from Nashville.

Belle Meade Plantation:

Just a short drive from downtown Nashville, Belle Meade Plantation offers a fascinating glimpse into the region's history and heritage. This historic site was once a renowned Thoroughbred horse farm and is now a museum showcasing the opulent lifestyle of the 19th-century South. Take a guided tour of the Greek Revival mansion, stroll through the beautifully landscaped gardens, and visit the onsite winery for a tasting of Belle Meade's award-winning wines. Learn about the plantation's role in the horse racing industry and explore the restored outbuildings that depict the lives of those who lived and worked on the estate. Belle Meade Plantation provides a captivating journey through time and an opportunity to delve into the cultural heritage of the region.

Mammoth Cave National Park:

For nature lovers and outdoor enthusiasts, Mammoth Cave National Park is a must-visit destination. Located approximately 90 miles north of Nashville, this vast underground labyrinth is the longest known cave system in the world. Embark on a guided cave tour to explore the intricate chambers, marvel at the stunning rock formations, and learn about the cave's unique ecosystem. Above ground, the park offers numerous hiking trails that wind through scenic woodlands and meadows, allowing visitors to appreciate the diverse flora and fauna of the area. Mammoth Cave National Park is a natural wonder that offers a truly unforgettable day trip experience.

Lynchburg:

Situated approximately 70 miles south of Nashville, Lynchburg is a small town known for its rich history and its famous Tennessee whiskey, Jack Daniel's. Take a guided tour of the Jack Daniel's Distillery to learn about the whiskey-making process, visit the historic buildings on the distillery grounds, and sample some of their signature spirits. Explore the charming downtown area, which features quaint shops, local eateries, and historic landmarks. Lynchburg is a delightful destination that offers a unique blend of Southern hospitality and whiskey heritage.

Land Between the Lakes National Recreation Area:

Located between Kentucky Lake and Lake Barkley, the Land Between the Lakes National Recreation Area is a vast expanse of protected land that spans over 170,000 acres. This outdoor paradise offers a wide range of recreational activities, including hiking, fishing, boating, and wildlife viewing. Explore the numerous trails that wind through forests and along scenic shorelines, visit the Elk & Bison Prairie to observe these majestic animals up close, or take a leisurely drive along the scenic byways to enjoy breathtaking views of the lakes and surrounding landscapes. Land Between the Lakes is a haven for nature enthusiasts and provides endless opportunities for outdoor adventure.

Lynchburg:

Situated approximately 70 miles south of Nashville, Lynchburg is a small town known for its rich history and its famous Tennessee whiskey, Jack Daniel's. Take a guided tour of the Jack Daniel's Distillery to learn about the whiskey-making process, visit the historic buildings on the distillery grounds, and sample some of their signature spirits. Explore the charming downtown area, which features quaint shops, local eateries, and historic landmarks. Lynchburg is a delightful destination that offers a unique blend of Southern hospitality and whiskey heritage.

Land Between the Lakes National Recreation Area:

Located between Kentucky Lake and Lake Barkley, the Land Between the Lakes National Recreation Area is a vast expanse of protected land that spans over 170,000 acres. This outdoor paradise offers a wide range of recreational activities, including hiking, fishing, boating, and wildlife viewing. Explore the numerous trails that wind through forests and along scenic shorelines, visit the Elk & Bison Prairie to observe these majestic animals up close, or take a leisurely drive along the scenic byways to enjoy breathtaking views of the lakes and surrounding landscapes. Land Between the Lakes is a haven for nature enthusiasts and provides endless opportunities for outdoor adventure.

Lynchburg:

Situated approximately 70 miles south of

Nashville, Lynchburg is a small town known for its rich history and its famous Tennessee whiskey, Jack Daniel's. Take a guided tour of the Jack Daniel's Distillery to learn about the whiskey-making process, visit the historic buildings on the distillery grounds, and sample some of their signature spirits. Explore the charming downtown area, which features quaint shops, local eateries, and historic landmarks. Lynchburg is a delightful destination that offers a unique blend of Southern hospitality and whiskey heritage.

Clarksville:

Located approximately 50 miles northwest of Nashville, Clarksville is a vibrant city with a rich history and a thriving arts scene. Visit the Customs House Museum and Cultural Center, which houses an impressive collection of art and historical exhibits. Explore Dunbar Cave State Park, home to a fascinating cave system and a variety of recreational opportunities, including hiking, fishing, and picnicking. Take a stroll along the historic downtown area, filled with unique shops, restaurants, and art galleries. Clarksville's combination of history, culture, and natural beauty makes it an ideal day trip destination from Nashville.

Natchez Trace Parkway:

Spanning over 400 miles from Nashville to Natchez, Mississippi, the Natchez Trace Parkway offers a scenic and leisurely drive through picturesque landscapes. The parkway follows the historic Natchez Trace, a trail that dates back thousands of years and was used by Native Americans, explorers, and settlers. Take a drive along the parkway to enjoy breathtaking views, stop at various historical sites and scenic overlooks, and explore the hiking trails that wind through the surrounding forests. The Natchez Trace Parkway is a serene and scenic route that allows travelers to connect with history and nature.

These day trips from Nashville offer a diverse range of experiences, from exploring history and culture to immersing yourself in nature and outdoor adventures. Whether you're seeking a taste of the region's rich heritage, a tranquil escape into natural beauty, or a chance to discover nearby towns and attractions, these destinations provide a refreshing change of scenery from the vibrant energy of Music City. So, pack your bags, hit the road, and embark on an unforgettable day trip adventure from Nashville.

Sports and Entertainment in Nashville

Nashville is not only a city known for its rich musical heritage but also a vibrant hub for sports and entertainment. Whether you're a sports fan looking to catch a game or a culture enthusiast seeking live performances and events, Nashville offers a diverse range of options to suit every interest. In this chapter, we will explore the sports teams, venues, and entertainment options that make Nashville a thrilling destination for sports enthusiasts and entertainment seekers.

Sports Teams and Venues:

Tennessee Titans (NFL):

Nashville is home to the Tennessee Titans, a National Football League (NFL) team that competes in the AFC South division. Catching a Titans game at Nissan Stadium, located on the east bank of the Cumberland River, is an exhilarating experience. The stadium's open-air design and state-of-the-art facilities create a lively atmosphere, allowing fans to cheer on their favorite team and soak in the excitement of NFL action.

Nashville Predators (NHL):

For ice hockey enthusiasts, the Nashville Predators, a professional ice hockey team in the National Hockey League (NHL), offer thrilling games at the Bridgestone Arena. Known for their passionate fan base and energetic game-day experience, the Predators bring the fast-paced action of hockey to the heart of Music City. Enjoy the camaraderie of fellow fans and experience the electrifying atmosphere of an NHL game at Bridgestone Arena.

Nashville Soccer Club (MLS):

Nashville Soccer Club represents the city in Major League Soccer (MLS), the top professional soccer league in the United States. Fans can catch their favorite team in action at Nissan Stadium or the newly constructed Nashville SC Stadium, a soccer-specific stadium located at the Fairgrounds Nashville. With the popularity of soccer on the rise in Nashville, attending a Nashville SC match promises an exciting and passionate experience for soccer enthusiasts.

Nashville Sounds (MiLB):

Baseball fans can enjoy America's favorite pastime by watching the Nashville Sounds, a Minor League Baseball (MiLB) team affiliated with the Milwaukee Brewers. The Sounds play their home games at First Horizon Park, a modern stadium located in North Nashville. With its scenic views of the city skyline and a family-friendly atmosphere, a visit to the ballpark provides an opportunity to enjoy a leisurely day of baseball while soaking up the vibrant spirit of the game.

Entertainment Venues and Events:

Ryman Auditorium:

Known as the "Mother Church of Country Music," the Ryman Auditorium is a historic venue that has hosted some of the biggest names in music. Located in downtown Nashville, this legendary music hall offers a unique and intimate setting for live performances. Experience the magic of a concert at the Ryman and witness the acoustics that have made it a beloved destination for musicians and fans alike.

Grand Ole Opry:

The Grand Ole Opry is a world-famous country music stage that has been showcasing the best of country music for over 95 years. Located at the Opryland complex, the Opry offers a one-of-a-kind experience to witness live performances from both legendary and emerging country artists. Immerse yourself in the rich traditions of country music and create lasting memories at this iconic venue.

Ascend Amphitheater:

Situated along the Cumberland River, the Ascend Amphitheater is an outdoor music venue that offers a scenic backdrop for concerts and live performances. With its open-air design and stunning views of the Nashville skyline, the amphitheater provides an intimate and immersive setting to enjoy a variety of musical genres and entertainment events.

Bridgestone Arena:

Apart from hosting Nashville Predators hockey games, Bridgestone Arena is a premier entertainment venue that attracts top-tier concerts, sporting events, and other live performances. From major concerts to family shows and championship sporting events, Bridgestone Arena offers a diverse range of entertainment options that cater to all interests.

Tennessee Performing Arts Center (TPAC):

For those seeking a diverse range of performing arts, the Tennessee Performing Arts Center is a cultural hub that hosts a variety of theater productions, ballet performances, concerts, and more. TPAC features multiple theaters, including the Andrew Jackson Hall, James K. Polk Theater, and the intimate Andrew Johnson Theater. Immerse yourself in the arts and witness world-class performances at this renowned cultural institution.

Music Festivals:

Nashville is renowned for its music festivals that draw visitors from around the world. The CMA Music Festival, held in June, showcases the best of country music with performances by top artists across multiple stages. The Pilgrimage Music & Cultural Festival celebrates a diverse range of music genres and features renowned musicians, local artisans, and culinary delights. These festivals provide an opportunity to experience the vibrant music culture of Nashville on a grand scale.

Broadway Honky-Tonks:

The honky-tonks on Broadway are a quintessential part of Nashville's entertainment scene. These lively venues offer live music performances throughout the day and night, featuring both up-and-coming artists and established acts. Enjoy the energetic atmosphere, dance to country tunes, and savor the authentic Nashville experience as you hop from one honky-tonk to another.

Nashville's sports teams, entertainment venues, and events offer an abundance of options for visitors seeking thrilling experiences and memorable entertainment. Whether you're a sports enthusiast, a music lover, or a fan of the performing arts, Nashville has something to offer everyone. So, plan your itinerary, secure your tickets, and get ready to immerse yourself in the excitement and entertainment that make Music City a destination like no other.

Art and Culture: Galleries and Artistic Spaces

Nashville is not only a city known for its music but also a vibrant hub for art and culture. From contemporary art galleries to creative studios, the city offers a thriving arts scene that showcases a diverse range of artistic expressions. In this chapter, we will explore the galleries, museums, and artistic spaces that make Nashville a destination for art enthusiasts and cultural connoisseurs.

Frist Art Museum:

The Frist Art Museum is a premier destination for visual arts in Nashville. Housed in a former post office building, the museum exhibits a diverse range of art from around the world, including contemporary and historic works. From thought-provoking exhibitions to educational programs and interactive installations, the Frist Art Museum provides a dynamic and engaging experience for visitors of all ages. Explore the museum's rotating exhibits, attend lectures and artist talks, and browse the well-curated museum shop for unique art-related items.

Cheekwood Estate and Gardens:

Cheekwood Estate and Gardens is a historic mansion that houses an impressive art collection and stunning botanical gardens. Explore the mansion's art galleries, which showcase a variety of visual arts, including paintings, sculptures, and decorative arts. Stroll through the meticulously landscaped gardens, featuring sculptures and outdoor installations that blend seamlessly with the natural surroundings. Cheekwood also hosts special exhibitions, art festivals, and outdoor concerts, making it a vibrant and inspiring destination for art and nature lovers.

The Parthenon:

Situated in Centennial Park, the Parthenon is a full-scale replica of the original Parthenon in Athens, Greece. This iconic landmark serves as Nashville's art museum and houses a permanent collection of American art from the 19th and 20th centuries. The centerpiece of the museum is a colossal statue of Athena, which stands at over 40 feet tall and is the largest indoor sculpture in the Western Hemisphere. Explore the galleries, learn about the history and mythology behind the Parthenon, and appreciate the architectural beauty of this cultural treasure.

The Arts Company:

Located in the heart of downtown Nashville, The Arts Company is a contemporary art gallery that showcases the work of local, regional, and international artists. With a focus on showcasing emerging talents and exploring new artistic expressions, the gallery offers a diverse range of contemporary art in various mediums. Attend gallery openings and receptions, engage in conversations with artists, and immerse yourself in the vibrant contemporary art scene that The Arts Company fosters.

Hatch Show Print:

Hatch Show Print is a historic letterpress shop and gallery that has been producing iconic posters since 1879. Known for its distinctive style and bold designs, Hatch Show Print has played an integral role in promoting Nashville's music and entertainment industry. Visit the shop and browse through their collection of prints, posters, and memorabilia, or take part in a guided tour to learn about the printing process and the shop's rich history. Hatch Show Print offers a unique glimpse into the art of printmaking and its significant impact on Nashville's cultural landscape.

Nashville Walls Project:

Nashville Walls Project is an initiative that brings renowned street artists from around the world to create large-scale murals and public art installations throughout the city. Explore the streets of Nashville and discover vibrant murals that add color and creativity to the urban landscape. The Nashville Walls Project not only showcases the talent of local and international artists but also contributes to the city's ever-evolving art scene.

Zeitgeist Gallery:

Zeitgeist Gallery is a contemporary art gallery that features works by both established and emerging artists. Located in the Wedgewood-Houston neighborhood, the gallery exhibits a diverse range of artistic expressions, including painting, sculpture, photography, and multimedia installations. Zeitgeist Gallery hosts regular exhibitions, artist talks, and events that provide opportunities to engage with the local art community and explore the latest trends in contemporary art.

Wedgewood-Houston Art Crawl:

The Wedgewood-Houston neighborhood is home to a vibrant art community and hosts a monthly art crawl, where galleries, studios, and creative spaces open their doors to the public. Join the art crawl to discover the works of local artists, explore the neighborhood's art venues, and engage in conversations with artists and fellow art enthusiasts. The Wedgewood-Houston Art Crawl offers an immersive and interactive experience that highlights the diversity and vitality of Nashville's art scene.

Nashville's art galleries, museums, and creative spaces provide a platform for artistic expression and cultural exploration. Whether you're a seasoned art enthusiast or simply appreciate the beauty of creative endeavors, the city offers a wealth of opportunities to engage with visual arts, contemporary expressions, and cultural heritage. So, immerse yourself in the vibrant art and cultural scene of Nashville, explore the galleries, attend events and exhibitions, and witness the city's artistic spirit come to life.

Music History and Heritage in Nashville

Nashville, often referred to as the "Music City," is renowned for its rich music history and vibrant music scene. From country music to rock, blues, and beyond, Nashville has been a hub for musicians and music lovers for decades. In this chapter, we will delve into the music history and heritage of Nashville, exploring the iconic landmarks, museums, and venues that have shaped the city's musical legacy.

The Ryman Auditorium:

The Ryman Auditorium, also known as the "Mother Church of Country Music," holds a special place in Nashville's music history. Originally built as a tabernacle in 1892, the venue became the home of the Grand Ole Opry radio show in the 1940s and '50s. Legendary performers such as Hank Williams, Patsy Cline, and Johnny Cash graced the stage, solidifying the Ryman's status as a symbol of country music heritage. Today, the Ryman continues to host concerts and events, offering visitors a chance to experience the magic of live music in an iconic setting.

Country Music Hall of Fame and Museum:

The Country Music Hall of Fame and Museum is a must-visit destination for any music enthusiast. Located in downtown Nashville, this museum celebrates the history and evolution of country music through interactive exhibits, memorabilia, and recordings. Explore the exhibits that showcase the lives and careers of country music legends, from Hank Williams and Dolly Parton to Willie Nelson and Garth Brooks. The museum also features special exhibits that delve into different aspects of the genre, offering a comprehensive overview of country music's impact on American culture.

Music Row:

Music Row is a historic district in Nashville that serves as the heart of the city's music industry. It is home to numerous recording studios, record labels, and music-related businesses. Take a stroll along Music Row and soak in the atmosphere where countless hit songs have been written and recorded. Visit the Owen Bradley Park, named after the influential producer, to pay homage to his contributions to the Nashville sound. Music Row offers a glimpse into the behind-the-scenes world of the music industry and the creative process that has shaped Nashville's music heritage.

RCA Studio B:

Located on Music Row, RCA Studio B is a historic recording studio that played a pivotal role in shaping the sound of country and popular music. Known as the "Home of 1,000 Hits," this studio has hosted legendary artists such as Elvis Presley, Dolly Parton, and the Everly Brothers. Take a guided tour of the studio to learn about its rich history, step into the recording booth where iconic songs were brought to life, and experience the acoustics that made Studio B a favorite among artists and producers.

The Johnny Cash Museum:

Dedicated to the life and music of the iconic "Man in Black," the Johnny Cash Museum offers a comprehensive look into the career and legacy of one of country music's most influential figures. Located in downtown Nashville, the museum houses a vast collection of memorabilia, including costumes, guitars, handwritten lyrics, and personal artifacts. Explore the exhibits that trace Cash's journey from his humble beginnings to international stardom, and gain insight into his impact on American music and culture.

Musicians Hall of Fame and Museum:

The Musicians Hall of Fame and Museum celebrates the talented musicians and session players who have contributed to some of the most iconic recordings in music history. Located in downtown Nashville, the museum showcases a collection of instruments, memorabilia, and artifacts that highlight the behind-the-scenes contributions of these unsung heroes. Discover the stories behind the musicians who shaped the sound of countless hit songs and learn about their lasting impact on popular music.

Honky Tonk Highway:

Broadway, also known as the "Honky Tonk Highway," is a vibrant street in downtown Nashville lined with iconic honky-tonks and live music venues. Step into these legendary establishments, such as Tootsie's Orchid Lounge and Robert's Western World, and immerse yourself in the lively atmosphere of Nashville's live music scene. Experience the energy of local bands playing traditional country music, rock 'n' roll, and everything in between. The Honky Tonk Highway is a testament to the city's ongoing commitment to live music and its vibrant nightlife.

The Bluebird Cafe:

The Bluebird Cafe is an intimate venue that has played a significant role in nurturing songwriters and showcasing their talents. Located in a nondescript strip mall, this small venue has hosted some of the most celebrated songwriters in the world, including Taylor Swift, Garth Brooks, and Kathy Mattea. Attend a show at the Bluebird Cafe and witness the magic of raw songwriting and captivating performances in an intimate setting.

Nashville's music history and heritage permeate every corner of the city, shaping its identity as the "Music City." From the iconic venues and museums that honor the legends of country music to the bustling live music scene on Broadway, Nashville offers a wealth of experiences for music lovers and history enthusiasts alike. Immerse yourself in the sights and sounds of Music City, trace the footsteps of musical legends, and celebrate the rich cultural heritage that has made Nashville a global destination for music aficionados.

LGBTQ+ Nashville: A Vibrant Community

Nashville is not only a city of music and culture but also a welcoming and inclusive destination for the LGBTQ+ community. With its vibrant nightlife, diverse community organizations, and numerous LGBTQ+-friendly establishments, Nashville offers a warm and inclusive environment for travelers of all identities. In this chapter, we will explore the LGBTQ+ scene in Nashville, highlighting the diverse array of attractions, events, and resources that make the city a thriving hub for the community.

LGBTQ+ Neighborhoods:

Nashville is a city where LGBTQ+ residents and visitors can find welcoming spaces throughout the metro area. While there isn't a designated LGBTQ+ neighborhood, areas such as East Nashville, Five Points, and Midtown are known for their inclusivity and LGBTQ+-friendly establishments. Explore these neighborhoods and discover a vibrant mix of LGBTQ+-owned businesses, bars, clubs, and community spaces that create a welcoming atmosphere for all.

Nashville Pride:

Nashville Pride is an annual celebration that brings together the LGBTQ+ community and its allies for a weekend of festivities, live entertainment, and advocacy. The event takes place in June, coinciding with Pride Month, and features a colorful parade, a diverse lineup of performers, community vendors, and educational exhibits. Nashville Pride serves as a platform to celebrate LGBTQ+ identity, raise awareness, and promote equality and acceptance within the community and beyond.

LGBTQ+ Bars and Nightlife:

Nashville boasts a lively LGBTQ+ nightlife scene, with a range of bars and clubs that cater to diverse tastes. Play Dance Bar is a popular destination for dancing and drag shows, while Tribe offers a laid-back atmosphere and diverse crowd. Lipstick Lounge provides a welcoming space for lesbians and their allies, and Canvas Lounge features regular LGBTQ+ events and themed nights. These venues, among others, offer a place for the community to socialize, express themselves, and celebrate their identities.

Nashville LGBTQ+ Community Center:

The Nashville LGBTQ+ Community Center serves as a hub for LGBTQ+ resources, support, and events in the city. Located in East Nashville, the center offers a variety of programs and services, including support groups, educational workshops, and social events. It also hosts community gatherings, art exhibitions, and discussion panels, providing a space for connection, advocacy, and empowerment within the LGBTQ+ community.

LGBTQ+ Friendly Businesses and Services:

Nashville is home to a wide range of LGBTQ+-friendly businesses and services that cater to the needs and interests of the community. From LGBTQ+-owned restaurants and shops to LGBTQ+-friendly healthcare providers and legal services, the city offers a welcoming environment where individuals can access inclusive services that respect their identities and support their well-being.

Queer Arts and Culture:

Nashville's art and cultural scene also embrace the LGBTQ+ community, with numerous events and spaces dedicated to showcasing queer art and fostering inclusivity. The annual Tennessee Queer Arts Festival celebrates LGBTQ+ creativity through a variety of artistic mediums, including visual arts, theater, music, and film. Additionally, art galleries such as the Red Arrow Gallery and the Julia Martin Gallery feature works by queer artists, providing a platform for their voices and experiences to be heard.

LGBTQ+-Friendly Accommodations:

Nashville offers a range of LGBTQ+-friendly accommodations where travelers can feel comfortable and accepted. From boutique hotels to LGBTQ+-owned bed and breakfasts, there are plenty of options to choose from. Many establishments proudly display their inclusivity and commitment to creating a safe and welcoming environment for LGBTQ+ guests.

LGBTQ+ Support and Advocacy Organizations:

Nashville is home to several LGBTQ+ support

and advocacy organizations that work tirelessly to promote equality, provide resources, and foster a sense of community. Organizations such as the Nashville LGBT Chamber of Commerce, the Tennessee Equality Project, and the Oasis Center's Just Us program offer support, networking opportunities, and advocacy initiatives to address the unique needs and challenges faced by the LGBTQ+ community.

Nashville's vibrant LGBTQ+ community embraces diversity, celebrates individuality, and creates a welcoming environment for residents and visitors alike. The city's inclusive spirit, diverse array of LGBTQ+-friendly establishments, and supportive resources make it an inviting destination for all who seek acceptance and celebration of their identities. Whether you're attending Nashville Pride, exploring LGBTQ+-owned businesses, or simply enjoying the inclusive atmosphere of the city, Nashville offers a vibrant and supportive community that celebrates the diversity of the LGBTQ+ experience.

Honoring Civil Rights: Nashville's Significance

Nashville holds a significant place in the history of the civil rights movement in the United States. From pivotal events to influential leaders, the city played a crucial role in advancing the cause of equality and justice. In this chapter, we will explore Nashville's significance in the civil rights movement, highlighting key landmarks, museums, and institutions that honor and commemorate this transformative period in American history.

Woolworth on 5th:

Woolworth on 5th, located in downtown Nashville, is a historic site that played a prominent role in the civil rights movement. In 1960, a group of African American students from nearby colleges, collectively known as the Nashville Student Movement, staged a series of nonviolent sit-ins at the store's lunch counter. These demonstrations challenged racial segregation and discrimination, inspiring similar protests across the country. Today, Woolworth on 5th serves as a restaurant and museum, preserving the memory of the sit-ins and offering visitors a glimpse into the struggle for civil rights.

The Civil Rights Room at the Nashville Public Library:

The Civil Rights Room at the Nashville Public Library is a dedicated space that documents the history of the civil rights movement in Nashville and beyond. The room features exhibits, photographs, and artifacts that highlight the courageous individuals and significant events that shaped the fight for equality. Visitors can explore interactive displays, view archival footage, and engage in educational programs that promote understanding and dialogue about civil rights.

Fisk University and the Freedom Riders:

Fisk University, one of Nashville's historically black colleges and universities, played a crucial role in the civil rights movement. The university's students and faculty actively participated in protests and demonstrations, and Fisk's Jubilee Singers, a renowned a cappella group, helped raise awareness and funds for the movement. Additionally, the Greyhound Bus Station, where the Freedom Riders encountered violence and resistance, stands as a testament to the bravery and determination of those who fought for racial equality.

The National Civil Rights Museum at the Lorraine Motel:

Although located in Memphis, just a few hours away from Nashville, the National Civil Rights Museum at the Lorraine Motel is a significant destination for those interested in the civil rights movement. The museum is built around the preserved Lorraine Motel, where Dr. Martin Luther King Jr. was assassinated in 1968. Through immersive exhibits and multimedia presentations, the museum tells the story of the struggle for civil rights and pays tribute to the leaders who fought for justice and equality.

Nashville Freedom Rides Museum:

The Nashville Freedom Rides Museum, housed in the historic Greyhound Bus Station, commemorates the courageous acts of the Freedom Riders who challenged segregation in interstate travel. The museum features exhibits, photographs, and personal testimonies that shed light on the experiences and challenges faced by these activists. By visiting the museum, visitors gain a deeper understanding of the sacrifices made and the progress achieved in the fight for civil rights.

Civil Rights Tour:

Numerous tour operators in Nashville offer guided tours that focus on the city's civil rights history. These tours take visitors to significant sites, providing insights into the local struggle for equality. Knowledgeable guides share stories and anecdotes about the events that unfolded in Nashville, allowing visitors to connect with the city's civil rights heritage on a deeper level.

Jefferson Street:

Jefferson Street, historically known as the center of Nashville's African American community, played a vital role in the civil rights movement. The street was home to businesses, clubs, and venues that served as gathering places for the black community. Today, the Jefferson Street area is undergoing revitalization, with efforts to preserve its historical significance and foster economic development. Exploring Jefferson Street provides an opportunity to reflect on the past and celebrate the resilience and contributions of Nashville's African American community.

The Witness Walls:

The Witness Walls is an outdoor installation located near the Nashville Public Library that honors the unsung heroes and heroines of the civil rights movement. This powerful tribute features large-scale sculptures and engraved panels that depict individuals who fought for justice and equality. The Witness Walls serve as a reminder of the collective struggle for civil rights and encourage visitors to reflect on the ongoing work needed to achieve true equality for all.

By exploring these landmarks and institutions, visitors to Nashville can gain a deeper understanding of the city's pivotal role in the civil rights movement. From the sit-ins at Woolworth on 5th to the activism at Fisk University, Nashville's history is intertwined with the fight for equality. By honoring these stories and experiences, Nashville serves as a reminder of the progress that has been made and the ongoing work needed to ensure a just and equitable society for all.

Nashville's Architectural Gems

Nashville is a city that blends rich history with modern innovation, and its architectural landscape reflects this dynamic spirit. From historic landmarks to contemporary designs, the city is adorned with architectural gems that captivate visitors and locals alike. In this chapter, we will explore Nashville's architectural highlights, showcasing the diverse range of styles, periods, and influences that shape the city's unique character.

The Tennessee State Capitol:

The Tennessee State Capitol, located atop Capitol Hill, is a prominent landmark in Nashville. Designed by renowned architect William Strickland in the neoclassical style, the building showcases grandeur and elegance. Its impressive white limestone exterior, adorned with Corinthian columns and a gilded cupola, stands as a symbol of democracy and government. Visitors can explore the interior, which features intricate architectural details, historical artifacts, and a beautiful legislative chamber.

The Parthenon:

The Parthenon, situated in Centennial Park, is a full-scale replica of the ancient Parthenon in Athens, Greece. Designed as a temporary structure for the 1897 Tennessee Centennial Exposition, the building was so beloved by the community that it was eventually reconstructed as a permanent feature. The Parthenon serves as an art museum, showcasing a collection of American art from the 19th and 20th centuries. Its majestic columns and intricate friezes pay homage to classical Greek architecture, making it a must-visit attraction for architecture enthusiasts.

Union Station Hotel:

The Union Station Hotel is a historic railway station turned boutique hotel that exemplifies the city's commitment to preserving architectural heritage. Designed in the Romanesque Revival style by architect Richard Montfort, the building features an imposing facade adorned with turrets, arches, and ornate details. Step inside, and you'll find a beautifully restored interior that marries the grandeur of the past with modern amenities. The hotel's architectural charm and historical significance make it a popular destination for visitors seeking a unique and luxurious experience.

The Hermitage Hotel:

The Hermitage Hotel, located in downtown Nashville, is an iconic example of Beaux-Arts architecture. Designed by architect James Edwin R. Carpenter, the hotel opened its doors in 1910 and has since become a cherished landmark. Its distinctive facade, characterized by grand arches, ornate detailing, and decorative elements, reflects the opulence of the era. The Hermitage Hotel has played host to numerous notable guests throughout its history and continues to be an elegant destination for travelers seeking a touch of old-world charm.

RCA Studio B:

While not traditionally considered an architectural gem, RCA Studio B holds a significant place in Nashville's cultural heritage. Located on Music Row, the studio is renowned for its contributions to the sound of popular music. Designed by architect Harold W. Bradley in the 1950s, the building's unassuming exterior belies the creative energy within. Step inside, and you'll find a space that has witnessed the recording of countless hit songs by artists such as Elvis Presley, Roy Orbison, and the Everly Brothers. The studio's acoustics and innovative design continue to inspire musicians and producers to this day.

Ryman Auditorium:

The Ryman Auditorium is not only an iconic music venue but also an architectural treasure. Built in the late 19th century as a tabernacle, the building showcases Victorian Gothic Revival architecture with its pointed arches, intricate brickwork, and distinctive stained glass windows. Its historic charm and superb acoustics have made it a beloved destination for musicians and fans alike. A visit to the Ryman is an opportunity to appreciate the architectural beauty of this revered venue and experience the magic of live music in a truly remarkable setting.

The Pinnacle at Symphony Place:

Nashville's skyline has experienced a transformation in recent years, with the addition of modern architectural marvels. The Pinnacle at Symphony Place is one such example. Designed by architectural firm Pickard Chilton, the 34-story office tower stands as a striking symbol of contemporary design. Its sleek glass facade, angled roofline, and energy-efficient features have earned it LEED Gold certification. The Pinnacle serves as a testament to Nashville's growing stature as a center for innovation and progressive design.

Belmont Mansion:

Belmont Mansion, located on the campus of Belmont University, is a stunning example of Italianate architecture. Built in the mid-19th century, the mansion features ornate detailing, grand columns, and expansive verandas that evoke a sense of elegance and grace. The interior is equally captivating, with beautifully preserved period furnishings and exquisite architectural elements. Guided tours offer visitors a glimpse into the opulent lifestyle of the mansion's original occupants and the architectural splendor of the era.

Nashville's architectural gems tell the story of the city's history, creativity, and cultural heritage. From neoclassical grandeur to modern marvels, these structures invite visitors to explore the diverse architectural styles that have shaped the city's landscape. Whether admiring the historic landmarks, appreciating the modern designs, or immersing oneself in the unique ambiance of these architectural treasures, Nashville offers a rich tapestry of structures that reflect the city's ever-evolving spirit.

Events and Festivals: Celebrating Music and Culture

Nashville, the renowned "Music City," is not only a destination for music enthusiasts but also a vibrant hub for festivals and cultural celebrations. Throughout the year, the city comes alive with events that showcase the rich musical heritage, diverse arts, and cultural traditions of Nashville and beyond. In this chapter, we will explore the exciting events and festivals that take place in Nashville, offering visitors a chance to immerse themselves in the city's vibrant music and cultural scene.

CMA Music Festival:

The CMA Music Festival is one of the biggest annual events in Nashville, drawing country music fans from around the world. Held in June, the festival features four days of live concerts, performances, and fan experiences at various venues across the city. Top country music artists take the stage, offering unforgettable performances and creating a festive atmosphere. Fans can also enjoy meet-and-greets, autograph signings, and interactive exhibits, making the CMA Music Festival an immersive celebration of country music and its passionate fan community.

Nashville Film Festival:

The Nashville Film Festival is an annual event that showcases the best of independent films and documentaries from around the world. Held in

October, the festival features a diverse lineup of screenings, panel discussions, and workshops. Film enthusiasts can enjoy a wide range of genres and themes, and even interact with filmmakers and industry professionals. The festival celebrates the art of filmmaking and provides a platform for emerging filmmakers to showcase their work, making it a must-visit event for cinephiles.

Bonnaroo Music and Arts Festival:

While technically held just outside Nashville in Manchester, Tennessee, the Bonnaroo Music and Arts Festival is a world-renowned event that attracts music lovers from across the globe. The festival, held in June, features a diverse lineup of artists spanning various genres, including rock, indie, hip-hop, and electronic music. In addition to the music, Bonnaroo also showcases visual arts, comedy performances, and immersive experiences. This multi-day festival creates a unique and vibrant community, making it an unforgettable celebration of music and arts.

Tomato Art Fest:

The Tomato Art Fest, held annually in August in the East Nashville neighborhood, is a quirky and colorful celebration of art and community. The festival pays homage to the tomato, showcasing local art, live music, and unique activities. Visitors can browse the art booths, participate in the tomato-themed contests, and enjoy live performances by local musicians. The Tomato Art Fest is a lighthearted and fun event that showcases the creativity and sense of community in Nashville.

African Street Festival:

The African Street Festival, held in Hadley Park in September, celebrates the rich cultural heritage of the African diaspora. The festival features live music, dance performances, food vendors, and arts and crafts displays. Visitors can experience the vibrant rhythms of African music, taste delicious African cuisine, and learn about the traditions and customs of various African cultures. The African Street Festival offers an opportunity to celebrate diversity and foster cross-cultural understanding in Nashville.

Music City Jazz Festival:

The Music City Jazz Festival, held in May, brings together acclaimed jazz musicians for a weekend of world-class performances. Jazz enthusiasts can enjoy smooth melodies, improvisations, and soulful rhythms in the beautiful setting of Public Square Park. The festival showcases both established jazz artists and emerging talents, creating an atmosphere of artistic excellence and appreciation for this iconic genre.

Nashville Oktoberfest:

The Nashville Oktoberfest, held in October, is the city's largest fall festival, drawing inspiration from the traditional German Oktoberfest celebrations. The event features live music, food vendors, arts and crafts, and plenty of beer. Visitors can sample German cuisine, participate in beer tastings, and enjoy live performances by local and international artists. The festival offers a festive atmosphere where people of all ages can come together to celebrate Nashville's vibrant culture and enjoy the spirit of Oktoberfest.

Tennessee State Fair:

The Tennessee State Fair, held in September, is a cherished annual event that celebrates the state's agricultural heritage, entertainment, and family fun. Visitors can experience a wide range of attractions, including livestock exhibitions, agricultural displays, amusement rides, live music, and food vendors. The fair provides a platform for local farmers, artisans, and performers to showcase their talents and products, offering an immersive experience that reflects the traditions and values of Tennessee.

These are just a few of the many events and festivals that take place in Nashville throughout the year. From music festivals that showcase diverse genres to cultural celebrations that honor traditions from around the world, Nashville offers a vibrant tapestry of events that cater to a wide range of interests. So, plan your visit accordingly and be prepared to immerse yourself in the lively atmosphere of Nashville's music, arts, and cultural scene.

Discovering Nashville's Coffee Culture

Nashville is a city that takes its coffee seriously. With a thriving coffee scene and an abundance of specialty coffee shops, the city has become a haven for coffee lovers. From artisanal roasters to cozy neighborhood cafes, Nashville offers a diverse range of coffee experiences that reflect the city's passion for quality and craftsmanship. In this chapter, we will explore Nashville's coffee culture, highlighting the top coffee shops, roasters, and unique experiences that await caffeine enthusiasts.

Bongo Java:

Bongo Java, located in the Belmont-Hillsboro neighborhood, is one of Nashville's oldest and most beloved coffee shops. Established in 1993, Bongo Java is known for its welcoming atmosphere, locally roasted beans, and quirky ambiance. The shop has gained a reputation for its creative latte art, including the famous "Nun Bun," a cinnamon roll that bears a striking resemblance to Mother Teresa. Whether you're enjoying a handcrafted espresso drink or indulging in one of their freshly baked pastries, Bongo Java offers a quintessential Nashville coffee experience.

Crema:

Crema, situated in the SoBro neighborhood, is a pioneer of Nashville's specialty coffee movement. With a commitment to ethically sourced beans and meticulous brewing techniques,

Crema has gained recognition as one of the city's premier coffee destinations. The shop's minimalist design, knowledgeable baristas, and innovative menu offerings create a space that celebrates the art and science of coffee. From single-origin pour-overs to velvety cappuccinos, Crema offers a sensory journey that delights coffee connoisseurs.

Barista Parlor:

Barista Parlor is a coffee institution that has garnered a cult-like following among Nashville's coffee enthusiasts. With multiple locations throughout the city, each shop features a unique aesthetic and atmosphere. Barista Parlor takes great pride in its meticulous approach to coffee, sourcing beans from top-notch roasters and utilizing precision brewing methods. The shop's vintage-inspired design, skilled baristas, and dedication to craftsmanship make it a must-visit destination for coffee lovers seeking a memorable experience.

Frothy Monkey:

Frothy Monkey is a neighborhood cafe that has expanded its footprint across Nashville. Known for its warm and inviting ambiance, Frothy Monkey provides a cozy setting to enjoy a cup of coffee and connect with the local community. The cafe sources its beans from ethical and sustainable farms, ensuring each cup is not only delicious but also socially responsible. In addition to coffee, Frothy Monkey offers a delicious food menu, making it an ideal spot for a leisurely brunch or a quick caffeine fix.

Headquarters:

Headquarters is a coffee shop and roastery located in East Nashville that caters to serious coffee aficionados. With an emphasis on small-batch, single-origin coffee beans, Headquarters offers a curated selection of meticulously brewed pour-overs and espresso-based beverages. The shop's commitment to quality extends to its minimalist design and attention to detail, creating an environment that showcases the pure essence of coffee. For those seeking a truly elevated coffee experience, Headquarters is a hidden gem worth discovering.

Dose:

Dose, situated in the Sylvan Park neighborhood, is a neighborhood cafe that has gained a loyal following for its consistent and delicious coffee offerings. The shop features a cozy interior, friendly baristas, and a menu that celebrates the diversity of coffee. Whether you're in the mood for a classic espresso drink or a refreshing cold brew, Dose offers a range of options to satisfy every palate. The cafe also serves delectable pastries and light bites, making it a go-to spot for locals seeking their daily dose of caffeine.

Eighth and Roast:

Eighth and Roast, with locations in the Eighth Avenue South and Sylvan Park neighborhoods, is a specialty coffee shop and roastery that focuses on small-batch roasting and precise brewing techniques. With a commitment to sourcing exceptional beans and fostering direct relationships with farmers, Eighth and Roast offers a coffee experience that showcases the unique flavors and nuances of each origin. The shop's minimalist aesthetic, knowledgeable staff, and dedication to quality make it a destination for coffee purists.

Nashville Coffee Festival:

For coffee enthusiasts visiting Nashville, the Nashville Coffee Festival is a must-attend event. Held annually, this festival brings together coffee roasters, baristas, and coffee lovers from near and far. Attendees can explore a variety of coffee tasting experiences, attend educational workshops, and engage in lively discussions about all things coffee. The festival also showcases local food vendors, live music, and interactive exhibits, creating a vibrant celebration of Nashville's thriving coffee culture.

Nashville's coffee culture is a reflection of the city's commitment to quality, community, and innovation. Whether you're seeking a cozy neighborhood cafe, an artisanal coffee roaster, or an immersive coffee festival, Nashville offers a diverse array of options to satisfy your caffeine cravings. So, embark on a coffee adventure, explore the city's coffee shops, strike up conversations with passionate baristas, and savor the flavors of Nashville's vibrant coffee scene.

Wellness and Relaxation: Spas and Retreats

In the bustling city of Nashville, finding moments of tranquility and rejuvenation is essential for visitors seeking a break from the lively atmosphere. Fortunately, Nashville offers a range of luxurious spas and wellness retreats that provide a haven for relaxation and self-care. From indulgent treatments to serene environments, these establishments cater to the well-being of both locals and travelers. In this chapter, we will explore the wellness and relaxation options in Nashville, allowing you to unwind and rejuvenate during your visit.

The Spa at Omni Nashville Hotel:

Situated in the heart of downtown Nashville, The Spa at Omni Nashville Hotel offers a sanctuary of relaxation amidst the vibrant city. The spa features a variety of soothing treatments, including massages, facials, and body scrubs, designed to melt away stress and promote overall well-being. The tranquil environment, coupled with skilled therapists and luxurious amenities, provides a pampering experience that rejuvenates both the body and mind.

Escape Day Spa and Salon:

Escape Day Spa and Salon, located in the trendy Green Hills neighborhood, provides a serene retreat for those seeking relaxation and rejuvenation. The spa offers a comprehensive range of services, including massages, facials, body treatments, and nail care. Their experienced therapists customize treatments to meet individual needs, ensuring a personalized and blissful experience. With its elegant ambiance and commitment to excellence, Escape Day Spa and Salon invites guests to unwind and escape from the demands of everyday life.

The Woodhouse Day Spa:

The Woodhouse Day Spa, situated in the Belle Meade neighborhood, is renowned for its luxurious treatments and tranquil ambiance. Step into this award-winning spa and embark on a journey of relaxation and indulgence. From soothing massages and rejuvenating facials to invigorating body treatments and hydrotherapy baths, The Woodhouse Day Spa offers a comprehensive menu of services to cater to your wellness needs. The serene atmosphere and attention to detail make it an ideal destination for those seeking a blissful escape.

Relache Spa at Gaylord Opryland Resort:

Located within the Gaylord Opryland Resort, the Relache Spa is an expansive oasis of relaxation and well-being. The spa features a wide range of treatments, including massages, body wraps, facials, and salon services. Guests can also enjoy the spa's luxurious amenities, such as steam rooms, saunas, and whirlpools. With its serene indoor gardens and tranquil atmosphere, Relache Spa offers a peaceful retreat from the vibrant energy of the resort and the city beyond.

Rhapsody Spa at the Westin Nashville:

Nestled within the luxurious Westin Nashville hotel, Rhapsody Spa provides a rejuvenating escape from the urban hustle and bustle. The spa offers a variety of treatments, including massages, facials, and body therapies, designed to enhance relaxation and well-being. Guests can also enjoy the spa's rooftop pool, offering stunning views of the city skyline. Rhapsody Spa invites visitors to unwind, recharge, and restore their mind and body in a serene setting.

Blooma Nashville Yoga:

For those seeking a holistic approach to wellness, Blooma Nashville Yoga offers a range of yoga classes and wellness services. Located in the 12 South neighborhood, this welcoming studio provides a space for practitioners of all levels to connect with their bodies and find inner balance. In addition to yoga classes, Blooma offers prenatal and postnatal yoga, as well as workshops and wellness services such as massage therapy and acupuncture. Immerse yourself in the nurturing environment of Blooma Nashville Yoga and embrace the healing power of movement and mindfulness.

Salt MedSpa of Nashville:

Salt MedSpa of Nashville offers a unique wellness experience centered around salt therapy. This holistic therapy involves relaxing in a room infused with pure salt particles, creating a serene environment that promotes respiratory health, reduces stress, and improves overall well-being. In addition to salt therapy, the spa offers other services such as infrared sauna sessions and massage therapy. Salt MedSpa provides a tranquil retreat where guests can revitalize their bodies and minds in a therapeutic and natural setting.

Tranquil Mind and Body Wellness Spa:

Tranquil Mind and Body Wellness Spa, located in the Berry Hill neighborhood, specializes in holistic therapies that promote relaxation and self-care. The spa offers a variety of services, including massage therapy, energy healing, and spa treatments. Guests can customize their experience by choosing from an array of treatments that address specific needs and preferences. With its serene ambiance and focus on holistic well-being, Tranquil Mind and Body Wellness Spa provides a nurturing space for rejuvenation and self-discovery.

Nashville's spas and wellness retreats offer a respite from the fast-paced energy of the city, allowing visitors to prioritize self-care and relaxation. Whether you seek a luxurious spa experience, a serene yoga class, or a holistic therapy, Nashville provides a range of options to cater to your well-being. Take time during your visit to indulge in these rejuvenating experiences and embrace the opportunity to recharge your mind, body, and spirit in the vibrant and thriving city of Nashville.

Uncovering Nashville's Haunted Places

Nashville, known for its vibrant music scene and rich history, is also a city steeped in tales of the paranormal. From ghostly apparitions to unexplained phenomena, Nashville is home to a collection of haunted places that intrigue and captivate visitors seeking a spine-tingling experience. In this chapter, we will delve into the supernatural side of Nashville, uncovering the city's haunted history and exploring some of its most notorious haunted locations.

The Hermitage:

The Hermitage, the former home of President Andrew Jackson, is not only a historic landmark but also rumored to be haunted. Visitors and staff have reported encountering apparitions, hearing disembodied voices, and experiencing unexplained phenomena throughout the property. One of the most famous ghostly residents is said to be Rachel Jackson, the President's late wife, who is occasionally seen wandering the halls or sitting by her grave in the garden. The Hermitage offers guided ghost tours, providing an opportunity to delve into the eerie history and paranormal legends surrounding this iconic site.

Ryman Auditorium:

The Ryman Auditorium, known as the "Mother Church of Country Music," has a rich musical history and is believed to be haunted by the spirits of legendary performers. Visitors and staff have reported encounters with ghostly figures, inexplicable sounds, and a pervasive sense of otherworldly energy within the venue. Some claim to have witnessed the apparitions of Hank Williams Sr., Patsy Cline, and other renowned artists who once graced the stage. Whether attending a live performance or taking a backstage tour, the Ryman Auditorium offers a chance to immerse oneself in the haunting tales that surround this iconic music venue.

Printer's Alley:

Printer's Alley, a historic downtown district known for its nightlife and entertainment, is believed to be haunted by the spirits of past patrons and performers. Throughout the years, numerous establishments in Printer's Alley have reported ghostly encounters, including phantom footsteps, apparitions, and unexplained sounds. One such location is Skull's Rainbow Room, a renowned jazz club that is said to be haunted by the ghost of a former magician who performed there. Exploring the vibrant nightlife of Printer's Alley provides a chance to experience the lively atmosphere and potentially encounter the lingering spirits of its haunted past.

Union Station Hotel:

The Union Station Hotel, a historic railway station turned boutique hotel, is said to be haunted by the ghost of a young woman named Abigail. Legend has it that Abigail was a runaway who died tragically in the station and now roams the halls in search of her lost lover. Guests and staff have reported sightings of a ghostly figure in a flowing white dress and have experienced unexplained temperature changes and flickering lights. Whether staying overnight or visiting the hotel's popular bar and restaurant, guests can immerse themselves in the ghostly lore that surrounds this elegant establishment.

Belmont Mansion:

Belmont Mansion, a magnificent antebellum mansion located on the campus of Belmont University, has a haunting reputation tied to its rich history. Some claim to have encountered the ghost of Adelicia Acklen, the mansion's original owner, who allegedly roams the halls and manifests as a figure in a flowing white gown. Visitors have reported cold spots, mysterious footsteps, and the sensation of being watched while exploring the mansion's grand rooms and beautiful gardens. Guided tours of Belmont Mansion offer a glimpse into the opulent past and the potential encounters with its otherworldly residents.

Two Rivers Mansion:

Two Rivers Mansion, a stately mansion set in the Two Rivers Park, is rumored to be haunted by the spirit of a former owner, William Harding. Visitors have reported seeing apparitions, hearing footsteps, and feeling a distinct presence while exploring the mansion's rooms and grounds. Two Rivers Mansion offers guided tours and hosts special events, providing an opportunity to delve into the paranormal history and perhaps experience a ghostly encounter of your own.

The Bell Witch Cave:

Although located outside of Nashville, the Bell Witch Cave is an infamous haunted site that draws paranormal enthusiasts from far and wide. Legend has it that the Bell family, who lived in the area in the early 19th century, experienced terrifying encounters with a malevolent entity known as the Bell Witch. The cave, located on the former Bell family property, is believed to be a portal to the spirit world and a place where supernatural activity continues to occur. Guided tours of the cave and its surrounding area offer a chilling glimpse into the haunting tales and mysterious occurrences associated with the Bell Witch.

Haunted Nashville Tours:

For those eager to explore Nashville's haunted history, various tour companies offer guided excursions that delve into the city's paranormal legends and ghostly encounters. These tours provide an opportunity to visit multiple haunted sites, hear chilling stories from local guides, and potentially experience paranormal activity firsthand. Whether on foot or aboard a ghostly-themed bus, these tours offer a thrilling and immersive experience for those fascinated by the supernatural.

Nashville's haunted places offer a glimpse into the city's eerie past and the lingering spirits that continue to captivate visitors. Whether you're a believer in the paranormal or simply intrigued by ghost stories, exploring these haunted locations provides a unique and spine-chilling perspective on Nashville's history. So, venture into the supernatural realm, embrace the mystery, and discover the haunted side of Music City.

Volunteer Opportunities in Nashville

Nashville is not only a city of vibrant music, delicious cuisine, and rich history, but it is also a community that values giving back. Whether you're a resident or a visitor, there are numerous volunteer opportunities in Nashville that allow you to make a positive impact and contribute to the well-being of the city and its residents. In this chapter, we will explore various volunteer opportunities in Nashville, highlighting organizations and initiatives that welcome volunteers and provide meaningful experiences for those looking to lend a helping hand.

Hands On Nashville:

Hands On Nashville is a volunteer organization that connects individuals and groups with meaningful volunteer opportunities throughout the city. They offer a wide range of projects, including environmental conservation, education, community development, and more. From assisting in community gardens to mentoring youth, there are countless ways to get involved and make a difference. Hands On Nashville provides a platform for volunteers to connect with local nonprofits and engage in impactful work that addresses the city's needs.

Second Harvest Food Bank of Middle Tennessee:

The Second Harvest Food Bank of Middle Tennessee is dedicated to fighting hunger in the region. They rely on the support of volunteers to sort and pack donated food items, distribute meals to those in need, and assist with various programs. By volunteering at the food bank, you can contribute to the fight against hunger and help ensure that individuals and families have access to nutritious meals. Whether you have a few hours to spare or are looking for a long-term commitment, Second Harvest Food Bank offers opportunities for volunteers of all ages and skill levels.

Nashville Humane Association:

Animal lovers can make a difference by volunteering at the Nashville Humane Association. This organization is dedicated to finding loving homes for animals in need and promoting responsible pet ownership. Volunteers can assist with tasks such as animal care, adoption events, community outreach, and administrative work. By volunteering at the Nashville Humane Association, you can play a crucial role in improving the lives of animals and helping them find forever homes.

Friends of Warner Parks:

Warner Parks, consisting of Edwin Warner Park and Percy Warner Park, is a beloved natural oasis in Nashville. The Friends of Warner Parks is a nonprofit organization that works to protect and preserve these parks for future generations. Volunteers can participate in various activities, including trail maintenance, invasive species removal, and environmental education programs. By volunteering at Warner Parks, you can contribute to the conservation of these natural treasures and help ensure that they remain accessible and beautiful for all to enjoy.

Habitat for Humanity of Greater Nashville:

Habitat for Humanity of Greater Nashville is dedicated to providing affordable housing for families in need. They rely on volunteers to assist with construction projects, home repairs, and other initiatives. By volunteering with Habitat for Humanity, you can help build homes, transform neighborhoods, and create a positive impact on the lives of families in the community. No prior construction experience is necessary, as they provide training and guidance for volunteers of all skill levels.

Nashville Cares:

Nashville Cares is an organization that supports individuals and families affected by HIV/AIDS through various programs and services. Volunteers can contribute by assisting with client support, outreach efforts, fundraising events, and more. By volunteering with Nashville Cares, you can make a meaningful difference in the lives of those living with HIV/AIDS and help create a supportive community.

Oasis Center:

The Oasis Center is a youth-centered organization that provides a range of services, including counseling, education, and support programs. Volunteers can get involved by mentoring young people, leading workshops, tutoring, or assisting with administrative tasks. By volunteering at the Oasis Center, you can help empower and inspire Nashville's youth, providing them with the guidance and resources they need to thrive.

Metro Nashville Public Schools:

Volunteering in the Metro Nashville Public Schools is an opportunity to make a positive impact on the education and well-being of local students. Volunteers can assist with tutoring, mentoring, classroom support, and extracurricular activities. By dedicating your time and skills to the schools, you can help students achieve their full potential and contribute to the success of the education system.

These are just a few of the many volunteer opportunities available in Nashville. Whether your passion lies in community service, environmental conservation, animal welfare, or education, Nashville offers a wide range of organizations and initiatives that welcome volunteers. By getting involved, you can connect with the community, make a difference in the lives of others, and create lasting memories and friendships along the way. So, roll up your sleeves, embrace the spirit of volunteerism, and contribute to the vibrant and compassionate community of Nashville.

Shopping for Souvenirs: Unique Nashville Gifts

When visiting Nashville, it's only natural to want to bring home a piece of Music City with you. Fortunately, Nashville offers a plethora of unique and memorable souvenirs that capture the essence of the city's vibrant culture and rich heritage. From music-inspired memorabilia to locally crafted goods, there is something for everyone to commemorate their Nashville experience. In this chapter, we will explore the diverse shopping options in Nashville, highlighting the best places to find unique Nashville gifts and souvenirs.

Hatch Show Print:

Located in the Country Music Hall of Fame and Museum, Hatch Show Print is a historic letterpress print shop that has been creating iconic posters for musicians since 1879. Visitors can browse a wide selection of beautifully designed posters, postcards, and other printed materials featuring legendary musicians and iconic Nashville landmarks. Each print is a unique piece of art that embodies the rich musical heritage of Nashville, making it a perfect souvenir for music lovers and art enthusiasts alike.

Ernest Tubb Record Shop:

For those seeking vinyl records and vintage music memorabilia, a visit to the Ernest Tubb Record Shop is a must. Established in 1947, this iconic shop offers an extensive collection of country, bluegrass, and rock 'n' roll records, as well as CDs, books, and other music-related merchandise. Browsing through the aisles of records and discovering hidden gems is a nostalgic experience that allows visitors to take home a piece of Nashville's musical legacy.

Olive & Sinclair Chocolate Co.:

Olive & Sinclair Chocolate Co. is a local artisan chocolate maker that specializes in handcrafted, bean-to-bar chocolates. Their unique flavor combinations, such as sea salt and caramel or Mexican-style cinnamon, reflect the creativity and quality for which Nashville is known. Visitors can indulge in a variety of chocolate bars, confections, and drinking chocolates, all made with carefully sourced ingredients and traditional techniques. Bringing home a box of Olive & Sinclair chocolates is a delectable way to savor the flavors of Nashville.

Goo Goo Cluster:

A true Nashville institution, Goo Goo Cluster is a beloved candy bar that has been satisfying sweet cravings since 1912. Made with caramel, marshmallow nougat, roasted peanuts, and milk chocolate, Goo Goo Clusters are a delicious combination of flavors and textures. The Goo Goo Shop, located in downtown Nashville, offers an array of Goo Goo Cluster varieties, including limited-edition flavors and merchandise. Taking home a box of these iconic treats allows you to share a taste of Nashville's confectionary history with friends and family.

The Turnip Truck:

For those looking to bring home local flavors and artisanal products, The Turnip Truck is a specialty grocery store that showcases Nashville's thriving food scene. The store features a selection of locally sourced produce, meats, cheeses, and gourmet pantry items. Visitors can also find a range of unique Nashville-made products, such as honey, hot sauces, pickles, and preserves. Shopping at The Turnip Truck allows you to support local producers and take home a taste of Nashville's culinary delights.

Draper James:

Draper James, a boutique founded by actress Reese Witherspoon, offers a curated selection of clothing, accessories, and home decor inspired by Southern charm and hospitality. The Nashville location, housed in a beautifully restored bungalow, captures the essence of the city's vibrant style and offers an array of unique and fashionable items. From clothing with a touch of Southern flair to charming home decor pieces, Draper James provides a sophisticated shopping experience for those seeking Nashville-inspired gifts.

The Johnny Cash Museum Store:

Located adjacent to The Johnny Cash Museum, the museum store offers a wide range of Johnny Cash memorabilia and merchandise. Fans of the "Man in Black" can find an assortment of items, including t-shirts, albums, books, and collectibles that celebrate the life and legacy of this iconic musician. The store's carefully curated selection ensures that visitors can find the perfect gift to honor Johnny Cash's impact on Nashville's music scene.

Hillsboro Village:

Hillsboro Village, a charming neighborhood near Vanderbilt University, is home to a variety of locally owned boutiques and shops. Here, visitors can find unique Nashville gifts, including handmade jewelry, clothing, accessories, and home decor. The area's eclectic mix of shops and its proximity to the university create a vibrant and youthful shopping experience, where visitors can discover one-of-a-kind treasures that reflect the artistic spirit of Nashville.

These are just a few examples of the many shopping opportunities in Nashville. Whether you're a music enthusiast, a food lover, or a fan of local craftsmanship, the city offers a wealth of options for finding unique Nashville gifts and souvenirs. So, take the time to explore the vibrant shopping scene, support local businesses, and bring home a piece of Nashville's distinctive charm and culture.

Hidden Gems and Off-the-Beaten-Path Destinations

While Nashville is known for its vibrant music scene, delicious cuisine, and iconic landmarks, the city also boasts a collection of hidden gems and off-the-beaten-path destinations that offer unique experiences for intrepid explorers. These lesser-known attractions allow visitors to delve deeper into Nashville's diverse culture, uncovering hidden histories and embracing local treasures. In this chapter, we will venture off the well-trodden path and discover some of Nashville's best-kept secrets.

Shelby Bottoms Nature Center and Greenway:

Escape the urban bustle and immerse yourself in nature at the Shelby Bottoms Nature Center and Greenway. Located just minutes from downtown Nashville, this 960-acre park offers a network of scenic trails, wetlands, and wildlife habitats. Visitors can explore the park on foot or by bike, enjoying stunning views of the Cumberland River and the opportunity to spot diverse bird species. The nature center provides educational exhibits and programs that highlight the importance of conservation and environmental stewardship.

The Parthenon:

Nashville's Parthenon, located in Centennial Park, is a full-scale replica of the iconic ancient Greek structure. Often overshadowed by the city's music-related attractions, this architectural gem is a hidden treasure that should not be missed. Step inside the Parthenon to admire the breathtaking statue of Athena Parthenos, the tallest indoor sculpture in the Western world. The surrounding park is an idyllic spot for picnics, leisurely strolls, and even the occasional music festival or outdoor performance.

Fort Negley:

Nestled on a hilltop just south of downtown, Fort Negley is a Civil War-era fortification with a rich historical significance. Built by Union troops during the war, it offers panoramic views of the city skyline and serves as a reminder of Nashville's role in the conflict. Visitors can explore the fort's remnants, participate in guided tours, and learn about the African American laborers who played a significant role in its construction. Fort Negley is a hidden gem that provides a fascinating glimpse into Nashville's past.

Lane Motor Museum:

Car enthusiasts and history buffs will delight in a visit to the Lane Motor Museum, which houses one of the largest collections of European vehicles in the United States. Located just a short drive from downtown, this quirky museum showcases over 500 unique and rare cars, motorcycles, and other modes of transportation. From vintage microcars to eccentric prototypes, the collection spans decades of automotive innovation. The Lane Motor Museum offers a captivating journey through automotive history that is sure to impress visitors of all ages.

The Frist Art Museum:

While not entirely off the beaten path, the Frist Art Museum is a cultural gem that often flies under the radar. Housed in a beautifully restored art deco building, this art museum showcases a diverse range of rotating exhibits, from classical to contemporary art. Visitors can explore the museum's vast collections, attend interactive workshops, and participate in engaging educational programs. The Frist Art Museum offers a unique and immersive artistic experience in the heart of downtown Nashville.

Beaman Park:

For nature lovers seeking serenity and seclusion, Beaman Park provides a tranquil retreat just outside the city. This 2,000-acre nature preserve features pristine forests, wildflower meadows, and hiking trails that wind through scenic landscapes. Visitors can explore the park's network of trails, encountering diverse wildlife and enjoying breathtaking views of the surrounding hills. Beaman Park offers a peaceful escape from the hustle and bustle of city life, allowing visitors to reconnect with nature and savor the beauty of Tennessee's wilderness.

Tennessee Central Railway Museum:

Step back in time and embark on a nostalgic journey at the Tennessee Central Railway Museum. Located in a historic train depot, this museum showcases a collection of vintage locomotives, passenger cars, and railway artifacts.

Visitors can take a ride on one of the museum's restored trains, immersing themselves in the golden age of rail travel. The Tennessee Central Railway Museum offers a unique and captivating experience that appeals to train enthusiasts and history lovers alike.

The Johnny Cash Farm:

Located in nearby Bon Aqua, the Johnny Cash Farm is a hidden gem for fans of the legendary musician. This peaceful retreat was once owned by Johnny Cash and served as a place of inspiration and respite for the "Man in Black." Visitors can explore the grounds, visit the cabin where Cash wrote some of his most famous songs, and learn about his connection to the property. The Johnny Cash Farm offers a glimpse into the personal life of one of country music's greatest icons, allowing fans to connect with his legacy in an intimate setting.

These hidden gems and off-the-beaten-path destinations in Nashville offer a chance to discover a side of the city that is often overlooked. Whether exploring the great outdoors, immersing yourself in history, or embracing cultural treasures, these lesser-known attractions provide unique and memorable experiences for adventurous travelers. So, venture beyond the well-known landmarks, uncover the hidden gems of Nashville, and create a truly extraordinary journey through Music City.

Tips for Traveling with Pets in Nashville

Traveling with pets can be a rewarding and enjoyable experience, especially when exploring a pet-friendly city like Nashville. With its welcoming atmosphere and numerous pet-friendly establishments, Music City provides ample opportunities for you and your furry companion to have a memorable adventure together. In this chapter, we will provide you with valuable tips and insights on traveling with pets in Nashville, ensuring a smooth and enjoyable experience for both you and your four-legged friend.

Pet-Friendly Accommodations:

When planning your trip to Nashville, ensure you choose a pet-friendly accommodation that caters to the needs of both you and your pet. Many hotels in Nashville welcome pets, but it's always best to check their pet policies, any size restrictions, and additional fees beforehand. Additionally, consider alternative accommodation options such as vacation rentals or pet-friendly bed and breakfasts, which may provide a more comfortable and home-like environment for you and your pet.

Research Pet-Friendly Activities:

Nashville offers a variety of pet-friendly activities and attractions that you and your furry friend can enjoy together. Research and plan ahead to find parks, hiking trails, and outdoor spaces that allow dogs on-leash. Some popular pet-friendly attractions include Centennial Dog Park, Warner Parks, and the Shelby Dog Park. These places provide ample space for your pet to stretch their legs, explore, and socialize with other dogs.

Visit Pet-Friendly Restaurants and Cafes:

Nashville's culinary scene is not just for humans; many restaurants and cafes welcome well-behaved pets on their outdoor patios. While exploring the city, take advantage of the pet-friendly establishments that allow you to enjoy a meal or a cup of coffee while your pet relaxes by your side. Some popular pet-friendly dining options include Bongo Java, TailGate Brewery, and The Dog Spot. Just remember to keep your pet leashed, well-behaved, and considerate of other patrons.

Plan Pet-Friendly Excursions:

Nashville offers more than just music and food; there are several pet-friendly excursions that you and your furry friend can partake in. Consider a pet-friendly riverboat cruise along the Cumberland River, where you can enjoy scenic views of the city while your pet basks in the fresh air. Additionally, some companies offer pet-friendly guided tours, allowing you to explore the city's history, architecture, or even its haunted side, all while keeping your pet entertained and engaged.

Pack Pet Essentials:

When traveling with pets, it's important to pack their essentials to ensure their comfort and well-being throughout the trip. This includes their food, treats, water, bowls, leash, waste bags, medications (if applicable), and a comfortable bed or blanket for them to sleep on. It's also a good idea to have a first aid kit specifically for your pet, containing items such as bandages, antiseptic wipes, and any necessary medications in case of an emergency.

Visit a Local Pet Store:

Nashville is home to several pet stores that cater to the needs of your furry friends. Take some time to visit these establishments to stock up on supplies or indulge in some retail therapy for your pet. Some stores even offer pet-friendly events or grooming services, allowing your pet to enjoy some pampering while in Nashville.

Be Mindful of the Weather:

Nashville experiences a range of weather conditions throughout the year, so it's important to be mindful of the weather when traveling with your pet. During hot summer months, avoid leaving your pet in the car, as temperatures can quickly become dangerous. Instead, opt for pet-friendly indoor activities or ensure you have a plan in place to keep your pet cool and hydrated. In colder months, provide your pet with appropriate winter gear, such as a coat or boots, to keep them warm and protected.

Find Veterinary Services:

While it's always ideal to have a healthy and happy pet during your travels, it's essential to be prepared for any unforeseen circumstances. Research and locate veterinary clinics or emergency pet hospitals in Nashville, so you have access to immediate care if needed. Keep important contact numbers and medical records easily accessible, and consider obtaining a temporary pet insurance policy that covers your pet while traveling.

Respect Local Regulations and Etiquette:

As a responsible pet owner, it's crucial to respect local regulations and etiquette when traveling with your pet in Nashville. Always keep your pet on a leash in public areas unless in designated off-leash areas. Clean up after your pet and dispose of waste properly. Be mindful of other people's comfort levels around pets and ensure your pet is well-behaved and under control at all times. By being respectful, you help maintain the pet-friendly environment that Nashville offers.

Traveling with pets in Nashville can be a rewarding and unforgettable experience. By following these tips, you can ensure a smooth and enjoyable trip for both you and your furry companion. Remember to plan ahead, research pet-friendly options, and prioritize the well-being and comfort of your pet throughout your Nashville adventure. Embrace the pet-friendly culture of Music City and create cherished memories together that will last a lifetime.

Music Recording Studios and Music Industry Insights

Nashville, also known as Music City, is a hub of creativity and a hotbed for aspiring musicians and industry professionals. With its rich musical heritage and thriving music scene, the city is home to numerous world-class recording studios where artists have crafted some of the most iconic songs in music history. In this chapter, we will explore the music recording studios in Nashville and provide insights into the city's vibrant music industry.

RCA Studio B:

RCA Studio B holds a legendary place in Nashville's music history. It was the recording studio where Elvis Presley, Dolly Parton, and countless other music icons laid down their tracks. Today, visitors can take guided tours of the studio and learn about its significance in shaping the Nashville sound. The tour offers insights into the recording techniques and equipment used during the golden age of music, allowing visitors to step into the footsteps of music legends.

Ocean Way Nashville Recording Studios:

Ocean Way Nashville Recording Studios is a state-of-the-art facility that has played host to recording sessions for renowned artists across various genres. The studio's expansive recording rooms, exceptional acoustics, and cutting-edge technology make it a sought-after destination for musicians and producers. While touring the studio may not always be possible due to ongoing recording sessions, visitors can still catch a glimpse of the iconic facility and learn about its contributions to the music industry.

Blackbird Studio:

Owned by legendary music producer John McBride, Blackbird Studio is a world-renowned recording facility that has attracted artists from all over the globe. With its impressive collection of vintage and modern equipment, as well as multiple recording rooms designed for specific sonic aesthetics, Blackbird Studio offers a versatile and inspiring environment for music creation. While access to the studio itself may be limited, visitors can participate in studio tours and gain valuable insights into the recording process and the studio's impact on the music industry.

Historic RCA Studio A:

RCA Studio A, also known as Historic RCA Studio A, is a historic recording space that has hosted sessions for some of the most influential artists in country music history. The studio has undergone several transformations over the years but has retained its unique charm and character. While not typically open to the public, special events and tours occasionally provide opportunities for visitors to step inside this iconic studio and learn about its historical significance.

House of Blues Studios:

Located in the Berry Hill neighborhood,

House of Blues Studios offers a professional recording environment with a laid-back atmosphere. The studio has attracted artists from a range of genres, including country, rock, and pop. While primarily a working studio, House of Blues occasionally opens its doors to visitors, providing a glimpse into the creative process and the behind-the-scenes workings of a professional recording space.

Sound Emporium Studios:

Sound Emporium Studios is another renowned recording facility that has contributed to the rich musical tapestry of Nashville. With its combination of vintage and modern equipment, spacious recording rooms, and a reputation for excellent sound quality, Sound Emporium has become a favorite choice for both established artists and up-and-coming musicians. While the studio is primarily focused on recording sessions, occasional tours and events offer visitors a chance to experience the studio's unique atmosphere and learn about its role in the music industry.

Music Industry Insights:

Beyond the recording studios, Nashville's music industry offers a wealth of insights and opportunities for aspiring musicians and industry professionals. The city is home to a multitude of music publishers, songwriters, producers, and record labels. For those seeking to learn more about the music business, Nashville provides a conducive environment for networking and connecting with industry insiders. Attending industry conferences, workshops, and events can offer valuable insights into the inner workings of the music industry and provide opportunities to showcase talent and build relationships.

The Country Music Hall of Fame and Museum:

While not a recording studio, the Country Music Hall of Fame and Museum is an essential stop for anyone interested in the history and legacy of Nashville's music industry. The museum showcases the evolution of country music, highlighting iconic artists, memorabilia, and the cultural impact of the genre. Visitors can explore exhibits dedicated to legendary musicians, songwriters, and industry pioneers, gaining a comprehensive understanding of the city's musical heritage and the contributions of its key figures.

Nashville's music recording studios and music industry insights provide a fascinating glimpse into the city's rich musical heritage and its continuing influence on the music world. Whether touring iconic studios, attending music industry events, or exploring the exhibits at the Country Music Hall of Fame, visitors can gain valuable insights into the creative process, the history of recording, and the business of music. Embrace the spirit of Music City and immerse yourself in the vibrant and inspiring world of Nashville's music industry.

Exploring Nashville's Riverfront and Waterways

Nashville, also known as the "Athens of the South," is not just a city of music and history; it is also a city of beautiful waterways and a vibrant riverfront. The Cumberland River winds its way through the heart of the city, offering a host of recreational activities, scenic views, and opportunities to connect with nature. In this chapter, we will explore Nashville's riverfront and waterways, providing you with insights and recommendations on how to make the most of these stunning natural assets.

Riverfront Park:

Nashville's Riverfront Park is a picturesque green space that stretches along the Cumberland River. The park offers stunning views of the river and the downtown skyline, providing a serene and relaxing atmosphere for visitors. Take a leisurely stroll along the riverfront promenade, relax on the grassy lawns, or have a picnic while enjoying the scenic beauty of the surroundings. Riverfront Park also serves as a venue for concerts, festivals, and events throughout the year, providing a lively and vibrant atmosphere.

Cumberland Park:

Located adjacent to Riverfront Park, Cumberland Park is a family-friendly destination that offers a range of interactive water features and play areas. The park's splash pad, climbing walls, and sandboxes provide endless entertainment for children, while the riverfront swings and picnic areas offer relaxation for the whole family. Take a walk along the park's trails, cross the pedestrian bridge, and enjoy panoramic views of the river and the city skyline. Cumberland Park is a delightful place to spend a sunny afternoon, offering a mix of water-based fun and natural beauty.

Riverboat Cruises:

One of the best ways to experience Nashville's riverfront is by taking a riverboat cruise along the Cumberland River. Several companies offer sightseeing cruises that allow you to enjoy scenic views of the city, learn about Nashville's history and architecture, and even enjoy live music performances onboard. Whether you opt for a leisurely daytime cruise or a romantic dinner cruise, exploring the river on a riverboat offers a unique perspective on the city and its waterways.

Pedestrian Bridge:

The John Seigenthaler Pedestrian Bridge, often referred to as the Shelby Street Bridge, is a landmark in Nashville and a favorite spot for locals and visitors alike. This historic truss bridge spans the Cumberland River, connecting downtown Nashville with the trendy neighborhood of East Nashville. Take a leisurely walk or bike ride across the bridge and soak in the stunning views of the river, the city skyline, and the surrounding areas. The bridge is particularly beautiful at sunrise and sunset, offering breathtaking photo opportunities.

Water Activities:

The Cumberland River and its tributaries offer a range of water activities for outdoor enthusiasts. Rent a kayak, paddleboard, or canoe and explore the calm waters of the river at your own pace. Several rental companies provide equipment and guided tours, allowing you to discover hidden coves, scenic backwaters, and even wildlife sightings. Stand-up paddleboarding is a popular choice, providing a fun and challenging way to explore the river while getting a workout. Whether you're a seasoned paddler or a beginner, Nashville's waterways offer endless opportunities for aquatic adventures.

Fishing:

Nashville's riverfront and waterways are a haven for fishing enthusiasts. The Cumberland River is known for its abundance of catfish, bass, and panfish, offering a rewarding fishing experience. Whether you prefer shore fishing or have access to a boat, cast your line into the river and enjoy the tranquility of the surroundings as you wait for a bite. Fishing permits and regulations apply, so be sure to obtain the necessary licenses and adhere to the guidelines set by the Tennessee Wildlife Resources Agency.

Bicentennial Capitol Mall State Park:

While not directly on the riverfront, the Bicentennial Capitol Mall State Park is a nearby destination that showcases the history and culture of Tennessee. The park features various monuments, fountains, and interpretive exhibits that highlight the state's rich heritage. Take a walk along the Pathway of History, which includes a representation of Tennessee's 95 counties, and learn about the significant events and individuals that shaped the state. The park's central feature, the Tennessee Capitol Building, offers a stunning backdrop for photos and provides a sense of grandeur.

Riverfront Events and Festivals:

Nashville's riverfront is a hub of activity throughout the year, hosting a variety of events and festivals that celebrate music, arts, and culture. From the Nashville Symphony's annual free concert on the riverfront to the Fourth of July fireworks extravaganza, there is always something happening along the river. Check the city's event calendar to see what festivals or activities coincide with your visit, and take part in the festivities to experience the vibrant energy and community spirit of Nashville.

Nashville's riverfront and waterways provide a refreshing escape from the city's bustling streets, offering opportunities for relaxation, recreation, and exploration. Whether you choose to stroll along the riverfront, embark on a riverboat cruise, or engage in water-based activities, you'll discover a different side of Nashville's natural beauty. Embrace the serenity of the water, enjoy breathtaking views, and make lasting memories as you immerse yourself in the enchanting riverfront experience that Music City has to offer.

Honoring Legendary Artists: Museums and Memorials

Nashville, also known as Music City, is a place deeply rooted in music history and the legacy of legendary artists who have made significant contributions to various genres. From country music icons to rock 'n' roll pioneers, Nashville pays tribute to these influential musicians through a variety of museums and memorials. In this chapter, we will explore the museums and memorials in Nashville that honor these legendary artists, providing visitors with an opportunity to connect with the rich musical heritage of the city.

Country Music Hall of Fame and Museum:

The Country Music Hall of Fame and Museum is a must-visit destination for any music lover. It serves as the custodian of country music history, preserving the legacies of artists who have made significant contributions to the genre. The museum features exhibits that showcase the evolution of country music, displaying artifacts, memorabilia, and interactive displays that bring the stories of legendary artists to life. From Hank Williams and Johnny Cash to Dolly Parton and Garth Brooks, the Country Music Hall of Fame celebrates the artists who have shaped the course of country music.

Musicians Hall of Fame and Museum:

The Musicians Hall of Fame and Museum honors the talented musicians who have played an instrumental role in shaping popular music across various genres. Located in the historic Municipal Auditorium, the museum showcases an extensive collection of instruments, stage outfits, and other memorabilia belonging to renowned musicians. Visitors can learn about the behind-the-scenes work of studio musicians, the significance of iconic instruments, and the impact of session players on the music industry. The Musicians Hall of Fame is a testament to the diverse talent that has emerged from Music City.

The Johnny Cash Museum:

Dedicated to the life and music of the legendary "Man in Black," The Johnny Cash Museum offers a comprehensive look at the iconic singer-songwriter's career and legacy. The museum houses a vast collection of memorabilia, including stage costumes, personal artifacts, handwritten lyrics, and photographs. Through exhibits and interactive displays, visitors can delve into Cash's musical journey, from his early days at Sun Records to his enduring impact on country and rock 'n' roll. The museum provides an intimate and personal experience, allowing fans to gain a deeper understanding of Johnny Cash's life and musical contributions.

Patsy Cline Museum:

The Patsy Cline Museum is a tribute to one of the most influential and beloved voices in country music history. Located within the Johnny Cash Museum complex, this dedicated space showcases personal artifacts, stage costumes, and memorabilia that tell the story of Patsy Cline's life and career. Visitors can immerse themselves in Cline's remarkable journey, from her humble beginnings in Winchester, Virginia, to her tragic and untimely death. The museum celebrates her enduring legacy and her impact on the genre of country music.

The George Jones Museum:

Located in the heart of downtown Nashville, The George Jones Museum honors the life and music of the iconic country music artist. The museum features exhibits that chronicle Jones's career, showcasing stage costumes, awards, and personal artifacts. Visitors can also explore the museum's rooftop bar, which offers panoramic views of the city skyline. The George Jones Museum provides an intimate and immersive experience, allowing fans to celebrate the life and music of one of country music's true legends.

The Buddy Holly Memorial:

Located in the Riverfront Park, the Buddy Holly Memorial commemorates the late rock 'n' roll pioneer's final performance, which took place in Nashville. The memorial features a life-size bronze statue of Buddy Holly with his guitar, paying tribute to his enduring legacy. Visitors can reflect on Holly's contributions to the music world and his influence on subsequent generations of musicians. The Buddy Holly Memorial serves as a reminder of the lasting impact of this iconic artist.

Hatch Show Print:

While not a traditional museum or memorial, Hatch Show Print is a historic letterpress print shop that has created iconic posters for musicians since 1879. Many legendary artists, including Elvis Presley, Johnny Cash, and Patsy Cline, have had their concert posters printed at Hatch Show Print. Visitors can take a guided tour of the print shop, witnessing the art of letterpress printing and browsing through an extensive collection of concert posters. Hatch Show Print pays homage to the artists who have graced the stages of Music City, leaving an indelible mark on the music industry.

These museums and memorials in Nashville provide a window into the lives and legacies of legendary artists who have left an indelible mark on the music world. From country music icons to rock 'n' roll pioneers, visitors can immerse themselves in the stories, artifacts, and music of these influential figures. Paying homage to the rich musical heritage of Nashville, these museums and memorials offer an opportunity to celebrate the artists who have shaped the course of popular music and continue to inspire generations of musicians and fans alike.

Discovering Nashville's Literary Heritage

Nashville, also known as Music City, is not just a hub of musical creativity; it has also fostered a vibrant literary community that has produced renowned authors, poets, and playwrights. From Pulitzer Prize winners to celebrated novelists, Nashville's literary heritage is rich and diverse. In this chapter, we will explore Nashville's literary scene, highlighting key literary landmarks, events, and resources that allow visitors to delve into the city's rich literary heritage.

The Southern Festival of Books:

The Southern Festival of Books is a prestigious annual event that celebrates the written word and showcases the work of authors from across the region. Held in downtown Nashville, this three-day festival features author readings, panel discussions, book signings, and literary performances. Visitors can engage with established and emerging writers, participate in thought-provoking discussions, and browse through a vast selection of books. The festival provides a unique opportunity to immerse oneself in Nashville's literary culture and connect with the vibrant literary community.

Parnassus Books:

Parnassus Books is an independent bookstore located in the Green Hills neighborhood of Nashville. Co-owned by author Ann Patchett, this beloved bookstore offers a curated selection of books across various genres. Visitors can browse through the shelves, attend author events and book signings, or seek recommendations from the knowledgeable staff. Parnassus Books is not just a place to buy books; it is a literary hub that fosters a sense of community and discovery, making it a must-visit destination for book lovers.

The Nashville Public Library:

The Nashville Public Library is not only a valuable resource for locals but also a treasure trove for visitors seeking to explore Nashville's literary heritage. The library houses an extensive collection of books, including works by local authors and volumes that delve into the city's history and culture. Visitors can spend hours browsing the shelves, conducting research, or simply immersing themselves in the tranquil reading spaces. The library also hosts author talks, workshops, and literary events throughout the year, providing opportunities to engage with the literary community.

The Fisk University Library:

The Fisk University Library is a significant institution in Nashville's literary landscape. Fisk University has long been associated with fostering creativity and intellectual pursuits, particularly within the African American community. The library holds a collection of rare books, manuscripts, and archives that highlight the contributions of African American writers and scholars. Visitors can explore the library's holdings, discover works by renowned authors such as W.E.B. Du Bois and Zora Neale Hurston, and gain insights into the city's rich literary and cultural heritage.

Literary Landmarks:

Nashville boasts several literary landmarks that pay homage to the city's renowned authors and their works. One such landmark is the F. Scott and Zelda Fitzgerald Museum, located in a historic home where the famous author couple once resided. Visitors can take a guided tour of the museum, learn about the Fitzgeralds' lives and literary achievements, and gain insight into the Jazz Age and its impact on American literature. Another notable landmark is the Belle Meade Plantation, which was the former home of acclaimed novelist Margaret Mitchell. Visitors can explore the plantation and learn about Mitchell's connection to Nashville and her iconic novel, "Gone with the Wind."

The Hermitage Hotel:

The Hermitage Hotel, a historic landmark in downtown Nashville, has played host to numerous renowned authors over the years. It has been a favorite spot for writers seeking inspiration and a quiet space to work on their craft. The hotel's Oak Bar has witnessed many literary conversations and gatherings, becoming a meeting place for authors and intellectuals. Visitors can enjoy a drink in this literary haven and imagine themselves surrounded by the literary giants who have graced its halls.

Literary Walking Tours:

Nashville offers literary walking tours that take visitors on a journey through the city's literary history and landmarks. These guided tours provide fascinating insights into the lives and works of notable authors who have called Nashville home or have been inspired by the city. As you walk the streets of Nashville, you'll discover the literary significance of various neighborhoods, visit the former homes of writers, and gain a deeper understanding of the literary fabric that weaves through the city.

Writing Workshops and Author Events:

Nashville's literary community offers numerous opportunities for aspiring writers and literature enthusiasts to engage with the craft. Writing workshops, author talks, and book signings are frequently held at bookstores, libraries, and community centers throughout the city. These events provide a platform for writers to share their experiences, offer insights into the writing process, and connect with fellow book lovers. Attending these workshops and events allows visitors to tap into the city's creative energy and gain inspiration from established authors and industry professionals.

Nashville's literary heritage is a hidden gem within the city's vibrant cultural landscape. From bookstores and libraries to literary landmarks and events, visitors can immerse themselves in Nashville's rich literary traditions. Whether attending the Southern Festival of Books, browsing the shelves of Parnassus Books, or exploring the city's literary landmarks, the literary enthusiast will find plenty of opportunities to celebrate Nashville's literary legacy. So, embrace the written word, discover the works of acclaimed authors, and let Nashville's literary heritage captivate your imagination.

Saying Goodbye to Nashville: Reflections and Memories

As your time in Nashville comes to an end, it's natural to reflect on the memories you've made and the experiences you've had in this vibrant city. Saying goodbye to Nashville is not just about bidding farewell to a travel destination; it's about carrying with you the spirit of Music City and the moments that have touched your heart. In this final chapter of our Nashville travel guide, we invite you to join us in reflecting on your journey and cherishing the memories you've created.

Soaking in the Music:

Nashville is synonymous with music, and throughout your stay, you've likely been serenaded by the sounds of live performances, honky-tonk tunes, and the soulful melodies that emanate from the city's countless venues. Take a moment to reflect on the musical experiences that have moved you, whether it was a memorable concert, an impromptu jam session on Lower Broadway, or the joy of discovering a hidden gem in a local bar. Let the melodies and lyrics linger in your mind as you bid adieu to Music City.

Embracing Southern Hospitality:

Nashville is renowned for its warm and welcoming atmosphere, known as Southern hospitality. From the friendly smiles and heartfelt greetings to the genuine conversations you've had with locals, you've experienced firsthand the genuine kindness and generosity of the people of Nashville. Take a moment to reflect on the connections you've made, the stories you've heard, and the bonds you've formed. Remember the moments when a stranger became a friend, and carry with you the spirit of Southern hospitality wherever your travels take you next.

Immersing in the History:

Nashville's rich history permeates the city, from its role in the Civil Rights Movement to its significance as a center for country music. Reflect on the historical landmarks you've visited, the stories you've learned, and the insights you've gained into Nashville's past. Remember the emotions you felt when standing in the footsteps of civil rights pioneers at the Nashville Civil Rights Room, or when exploring the exhibits at the Country Music Hall of Fame and Museum. Let the history of Nashville inspire a deeper appreciation for the city's cultural heritage.

Exploring the Culinary Delights:

Nashville's culinary scene is a treat for the taste buds, offering a wide array of mouthwatering dishes and Southern flavors. Take a moment to savor the memories of the delicious meals you've enjoyed, from hot chicken and barbecue to classic Southern comfort food. Reflect on the bustling farmers' markets, food trucks, and eclectic restaurants that have tantalized your senses. Consider the flavors that have left an indelible mark on your palate, and perhaps take some recipes or foodie inspiration back home with you.

Discovering Hidden Gems:

As you bid farewell to Nashville, reminisce about the off-the-beaten-path destinations and hidden gems you stumbled upon during your explorations. Recall the moments of awe when stumbling upon a vibrant mural in a quiet neighborhood, or the joy of discovering a quaint boutique tucked away in a side street. Cherish the memories of the unexpected encounters, the serendipitous discoveries, and the small moments of wonder that have made your time in Nashville truly special.

Gratitude for Nature's Beauty:

Nashville's natural beauty is a treasure to behold, from its sprawling parks and green spaces to the scenic waterways that wind through the city. Reflect on the moments of tranquility you've experienced while walking along the riverfront, exploring the trails in a local park, or simply admiring the vibrant colors of a sunset. Take a moment to express gratitude for the natural wonders that have provided moments of peace and serenity during your Nashville adventure.

Capturing the Spirit:

Nashville's spirit is a unique blend of creativity, resilience, and passion. Reflect on the spirit of the city that has touched your soul and inspired your own sense of creativity. Consider the art, music, and vibrant culture that permeate every corner of Nashville, and let the city's spirit infuse your own journey beyond its borders. Carry with you the determination and drive that Nashville embodies, allowing it to fuel your own pursuit of dreams and passions.

Planning Your Return:

Saying goodbye to Nashville doesn't have to be a final farewell. Take a moment to reflect on the memories and experiences that have made your visit special, and consider planning a return trip in the future. Nashville's ever-evolving music scene, cultural offerings, and warm hospitality ensure that there will always be new experiences to discover and new memories to create. Let your departure from Nashville be a "see you later" rather than a final goodbye.

As you prepare to leave Nashville, carry the city's spirit with you. Cherish the memories, the connections, and the experiences that have shaped your time in Music City. Reflect on the moments that have touched your heart and let them inspire you to embrace the next chapter of your journey. As you bid adieu to Nashville, remember that the city will always be there, waiting to welcome you back with open arms.

Milton Keynes UK
Ingram Content Group UK Ltd.
UKHW020829110424
440949UK00001B/116